Central City Malls

Central City Malls

Harvey M. Rubenstein

A Wiley-Interscience Publication
John Wiley & Sons
New York   Chichester   Brisbane   Toronto

Library of Congress Cataloging in Publication Data

Rubenstein, Harvey M.
  Central city malls.

  "A Wiley-Interscience publication."
  Bibliography: p.
  Includes index.
  1. Shopping malls. 2. Central business districts.
3. Pedestrian facilities design. 4. City planning.
5. Landscape architecture. I. Title.

HF5430.R8   711'.552   78-7536
ISBN 0-471-03098-8

Printed in the United States of America

10 9 8 7 6 5 4 3 2

To my parents

Preface

It is the purpose of *Central City Malls* to illustrate how pedestrian malls have become an exciting part of the revitalization of downtown business districts. Pedestrian malls have developed out of the need for renewing downtown shopping areas to compete with suburban shopping centers, to create a new image for a city, to increase retail sales, to strengthen property values, and to promote new investor interest. This book discusses the process of developing a mall, including feasibility analysis, planning, and design. The great interest in rebuilding downtowns, and the enthusiasm for the design and construction of malls, have also led to improved understanding of the problems that affect downtown areas.

In reviewing mall feasibility, cultural factors such as traffic, transit, and parking are analyzed, as well as natural factors like soils and climate, and economic factors like market analysis and cost benefit; the funding, political, and legal factors involved in the establishment of a mall are also explored. Readers will find that analysis of these factors determines a mall's feasibility, size, location, and cost.

This book also reviews the physical factors related to the context of a mall, such as image and form characteristics.

Design elements and street furnishings are also discussed and are shown photographically. These include items such as paving, sculpture, fountains, lighting, seating, and canopies.

The importance of trees in the city for climatic uses, environmental engineering, and architectural and aesthetic value is reviewed with specific examples of types of trees suitable for the city and mall.

To provide in-depth examples of full malls, semimalls, and transit malls, 22 case studies are illustrated for cities of varying size in the United States and Canada. These case studies cover mall description, development strategy, design features, and impact on sales, city image, and design quality. A catalogue of 90 malls is also presented in an appendix, with data on mall type, number of blocks, date completed, type of funding, cost, and sales impact.

Central City Malls, which evolved out of research for the Wyoming Avenue Mini-Mall in Scranton, Pennsylvania, will be of interest to architects, landscape architects, urban planners, and engineers who are involved in the planning and design of future malls, as well as to students of these professions and to public officials such as mayors, city managers, redevelopment directors, city council members, county administrators, and art and planning commission members involved in studying malls for their cities. In the area of business, members of chambers of commerce and other commercial associations, financiers, and developers who promote private investment will also find this book to be of value.

Harvey M. Rubenstein
Clarks Summit, Pennsylvania
June 1978

Acknowledgments

For their assistance in preparing this book, I wish to thank all those who provided information, including city planning agencies, urban renewal agencies, chambers of commerce, and downtown development groups. I am grateful also to the private architectural and landscape architectural firms that contributed information.

Special thanks are due to my secretary, Virginia Hrywnak, for typing the manuscript, to librarian Betsey Moylan, to Anthony Tellie for his help in preparing illustrations, and to Coral Lee Watson and my wife Toby for editing.

H.M.R.

Contents

6. CASE STUDIES

84

APPENDIX: Catalogue of Central City Malls

180

BIBLIOGRAPHY

187

INDEX

189

Central City Malls

1
Introduction

Traditionally the word "mall" has meant an area usually lined with shade trees and used as a public walk or promenade. As used today, "mall" denotes a new kind of street or plaza in central city business areas oriented toward pedestrians and served by public transit.

MALL DEVELOPMENT

There are many reasons for building a mall, the primary one being to revitalize an area of the central business district in a given city in order to increase retail sales, to strengthen property values, to compete with suburban shopping centers, and to encourage private investment by creating a stable environment for retail business. A mall also creates a new image for a city, generating a feeling of pride among residents and demonstrating that the city government and merchants are able to work together to improve their city. In addition, it creates new

(*Preceding page*)
Lexington Street Mall, Baltimore, Maryland. (Photograph courtesy of O'Malley and Associates, Inc.)

Antique car shows are held in Penn Square, Reading, Pennsylvania.

Children's play area, Central City Mall, Williamsport, Pennsylvania, by Miceli, Weed, Kulik, Inc.

(*Opposite page*)
View of Fulton Street Mall, Fresno, California. (Photograph courtesy of Gruen Associates.)

opportunities for the promotion of retail sales.

The mall becomes a place in which to improve the quality and variety of downtown activities. It provides a center for exhibits, concerts, fashion shows, flower shows, boat shows, antique car shows, parades, band concerts, arts and crafts festivals, and other events.

A mall also provides shaded areas in which to walk, sitting areas in which to relax, sculpture, fountains, children's play areas, outdoor din-

ing areas, and interesting paving and night lighting effects. A well developed mall therefore creates an improved physical and social environment for the block or blocks in which it is located and for adjacent areas as well.

MALL TYPES

The three major types of malls are the full mall, the transit mall, and the semimall. These malls offer a wide variety of designs.

Full Mall

A full mall is obtained by closing a street that was formerly used for vehicular traffic and then improving the pedestrian street or plaza with new paving, trees, benches, lighting, and other amenities such as sculpture and fountains.

Transit Mall

A transit mall or transitway is developed by removing automobile and truck traffic on an existing street and allowing only public

transit such as buses and taxis in the area. On-street parking is prohibited, walks are widened, and other amenities are added.

Semimall

In the semimall the amount of traffic and parking is reduced. The expanded pedestrian areas that result are provided with new trees and planting, benches, lighting, and other amenities.

Full malls have been built in areas with varying population sizes and economic bases. These have ranged from towns of 9725 residents, such as Lebanon, New Hampshire, to cities with populations of over 360,000, such as Louisville, Kentucky. Transit malls have been built in cities of even larger size, for example, Minneapolis, Minnesota; Portland, Oregon; Philadelphia, Pennsylvania; and Vancouver, British Columbia.

COST

Costs vary greatly in the construction of malls, depending on whether the mall is modest in scope or very comprehensive. In the latter case the complete reconstruction of utility lines and the incorporation of many outstanding amenities may be included in the design. The cost, for example, of constructing River City Mall in Louisville in 1973 was $1.7 million for a 3-block area, of constructing Nicollet Mall in Minneapolis in 1967 was $3.875 million

The Chestnut Street Transitway, Philadelphia, is an example of a mall where buses have primary access. (Photograph courtesy of Ueland and Junker.)

CENTRAL CITY MALLS

for 8 blocks, and of constructing the Chestnut Street Mall in Philadelphia in 1976 was $7.4 million for 12 blocks.

To achieve the most benefit for the money invested there should obviously be a balance between good design and cost.

The great interest in revitalizing central city areas and the enthusiasm for the design and construction of malls have also led to increased understanding of the problems that affect downtown areas. For example, when traffic and parking related to mall development are analyzed, it usually becomes apparent that, in order for a downtown mall to function, adequate parking must be provided within easy walking distance of shopping.

Parking and other factors affecting the feasibility of design of a mall are discussed in the following chapter.

Hamilton Mall, Allentown, Pennsylvania, has been developed as a four-block semimall by Cope, Linder, and Walmsley.

2 Feasibility Analysis

(*Preceding pages*)
View of informal sitting area at Main Street Mall, Charlottesville, Virginia.

To determine whether a mall can be developed successfully, a feasibility study must be carried out. This study analyzes all the factors—cultural, natural, socioeconomic, funding, political, and legal—that influence the development of a mall. Without a high quality feasibility analysis, there are insufficient data on which to base a sound decision about building a mall.

Upon completion of the feasibility study, the question of whether to build a mall is answered on the basis of the factual information contained in the analysis. If the decision is affirmative, the location, type, length, and cost of the mall are also derived from these data.

As the information is inventoried and analyzed, important factors should be illustrated graphically so that they may be easily understood by those reviewing the feasibility report, including the public, whose reactions may influence the outcome of the project.

The following checklist of factors

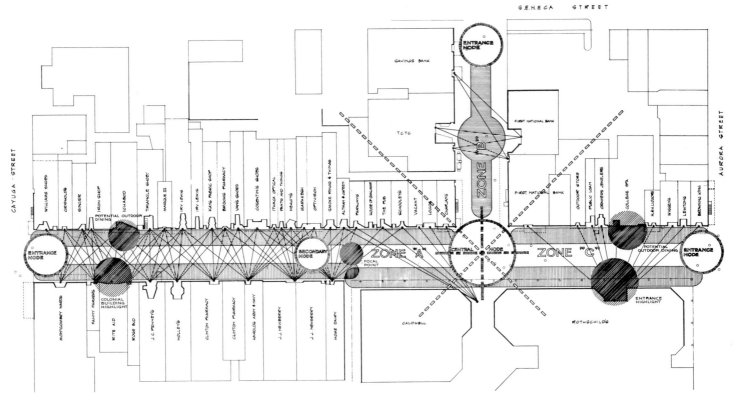

Site analysis, Ithaca Commons. (Photograph courtesy of Anton J. Egner and Associates.)

contains many of the items that should be reviewed to determine the feasibility of a proposed mall.

Cultural Factors

1. Traffic.
2. Transit.
3. Parking.
4. Service—trucks, emergency vehicles.
5. Pedestrian circulation—safety, security, origin and destination.
6. Utilities—storm drainage, sewage disposal, electricity, gas, water, steam, telephone.
7. Existing buildings—condition, height, architectural character, vaults.
8. Furnishings—signs, lights, street furniture.
9. Maintenance.

Natural Factors

1. Soils.
2. Climate.
3. Topography.
4. Water table.
5. Vegetation.

Socioeconomic Factors

1. Market analysis.
2. Cost/benefit.

Political, Funding, and Legal Factors

1. Approvals.
2. Federal, state, and local funding.
3. State and city laws.

CULTURAL FACTORS

Traffic

When a mall is proposed, the first question that usually arises is whether adjacent streets can handle the additional traffic. In some downtown areas these streets may already be overloaded with traffic. To determine the viability of placing a mall in a specific block or blocks,

it is necessary to measure the actual traffic volumes already utilizing the street or streets involved. This includes gathering data on the following:

1. Origin and destination of vehicles.
2. Average daily traffic volumes.
3. Peak hour traffic volumes—morning and afternoon.
4. Turning movement counts at all intersections.

"Origin and destination" denotes where traffic is coming from and where it is going. This information, as well as trip purpose, is obtained from interviews. To accomplish this, a cordon is circumscribed around the central business district (CBD) and traffic is counted entering and leaving. The survey on trip purpose is also carried out in this area. Once the desired traffic data for the proposed street location of the mall are obtained, a similar evaluation must be made for adjacent streets that would receive the diverted traffic. The data for the diverted traffic are then superimposed over the streets designated to receive it. If the data provided by the traffic study determine that in the present circulation system adjacent streets cannot handle the additional traffic, there may be alternatives. In some cases, for example, a revised one-way street system will eliminate turning movement at intersections, thereby increasing capacity during peak hours by simplifying the traffic signalization. Timing the traffic signals so that they are well coordinated also improves capacity. A bypass route also does much to resolve traffic congestion, although this may be a long-term alternative. The matter of developing a mall often raises further questions about the overall downtown circulation plan. The mall may therefore act as a catalyst to improve the overall downtown traffic pattern. This was the case in Fresno, California, where

a loop was provided around the entire downtown core and freeway routes were located 20 years ahead of the proposed construction dates. Proposing changes to the existing downtown traffic scheme is likely to elicit some public criticism. Usually, however, these complaints will cease after the mall is completed and the vehicular circulation problems are improved.

In some communities closing a block to traffic has been attempted as a test to see whether the adjacent blocks can handle additional traffic. This trial procedure has sometimes had positive results, as in the Sparks Street Mall in Ottawa, Canada (see p. 166). It does not work as well, however, if no other changes have been made to the block for improving traffic flow, and no amenities have been added. This was the case with the Hamilton Mall in Allentown, Pennsylvania (see p. 5), where a full mall had been desired at first. The trial results in unfavorable publicity for the mall idea if adjacent streets become overloaded, if on-street parking spaces are removed without other provisions for parking, and if bus routing is interrupted.

Traffic studies should be carried out under the direction of a qualified traffic engineer to ensure accuracy and comprehension. If a community has such an engineer on its staff, he will be able to coordinate and analyze the data; if not, a consultant should be retained.

Public Transit

Bus routes are another important area for study. Developing a full mall on a major block or blocks presupposes moving bus stops to other streets.

Changing a two-way street system to a one-way system may mean moving bus stops to the other side of the street. It may also involve relocating bus shelters or developing new ones. Bus stops in the vicinity of the proposed mall should therefore be inventoried.

Taxi service will also be affected if a full mall is developed. Taxi stands or drop-off areas may have to be developed on adjacent streets.

The impact of the mall in terms of traffic and transit must therefore be studied in its overall context, with consideration given to other streets in the area. These streets should be reviewed for parking, bus stops, taxi stands, and truck loading zones.

Parking

When a full mall or transit mall is constructed, parking spaces are removed. These spaces are generally also reduced or removed for a semimall. With parking in short supply in many downtown areas, the parking spaces must be relocated or added in areas within convenient walking distance of the mall. The mall may well generate a need for additional parking, or parking may have been inadequate even before the study was made.

One of the reasons for the success of the suburban shopping mall is the convenient free parking. If a downtown mall is to compete, convenient low cost parking is essential.

The city of Ithaca, New York, provides 45 minutes of free parking adjacent to the Ithaca Commons (see p. 8). Eugene, Oregon, provides unlimited free parking for shoppers.

If, in the downtown plan, it is determined that surface parking and

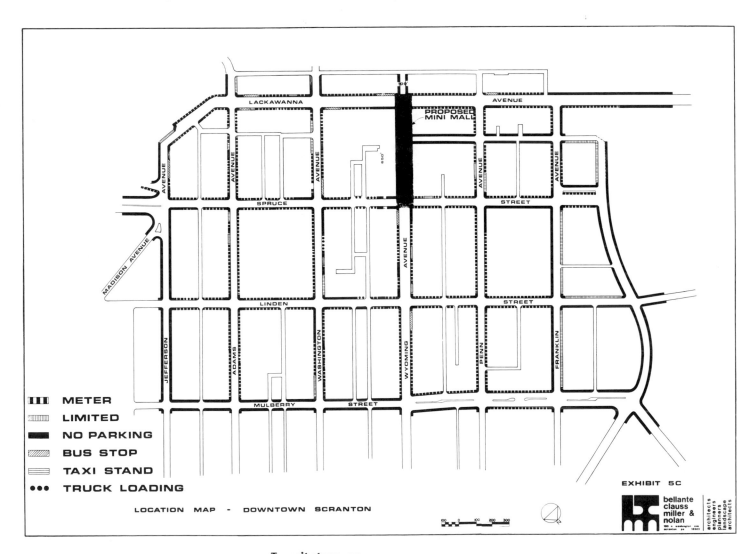

Transit stops, on-street parking, and truck loading are inventoried for a mall feasibility study for Scranton, Pennsylvania. (Photograph courtesy of Bellante, Clauss, Miller, and Nolan.)

curb parking are not adequate, multilevel parking structures should be considered. The economic feasibility of a parking structure is based on how much of the construction cost must be allocated for amortization and interest. At $4000 to $5000 per parking space, it takes about $1.50 per day per space just to break even. This means that the space will not carry itself on $0.10 per hour, or even $0.25 per hour in some cases. Revenue projections should carefully consider parking rate structure to obtain a realistic picture of income. All factors related to the design of the parking facilities, such as capacity, access, and layout, should be reviewed before financing is arranged. To help pay for a parking structure, and to keep parking rates in the new structure low, a form of financial assistance such as rental income from shops at street level, or balancing expenses by means of surface lots or curb meters already in existence, may be necessary.

Parking should be located in such a way as to minimize walking distance to the mall. One way to accomplish this is to develop parking lots or garages on streets parallel to the mall. Parking garages may also be built with pedestrian walkways bridging streets and leading directly into the mall. Sometimes parking is also located behind existing stores on the mall, and may be connected to the mall by walkways between buildings or linked directly to department stores.

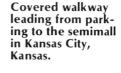

Covered walkway leading from parking to the semimall in Kansas City, Kansas.

Service and Emergency Access

In the development of a full mall, accessibility for service is a major functional consideration. Service vehicles include trucks for deliveries, shipments, and trash removal, and emergency vehicles such as ambulances, police cars, and fire trucks. When a block is closed to cars and buses, trucks are also barred. Is there an alternative means of access so that buildings can be served from alleys, back streets, or special loading zones?

A building-by-building survey of how services are currently handled must be made in order to review the feasibility of servicing the businesses when a mall is in existence. This study includes deliveries, shipments, and trash removal.

If the survey shows that servicing the buildings from service cores or alleys is not practical, it may be necessary to allow service vehicles on the mall for specified periods, such as 7:00 P.M. to 10:00 A.M. An alternative method may be to

develop a service lane through the mall.

Room must also be provided for emergency vehicles such as police cars, ambulances, and fire fighting equipment. Usually a 15-foot-wide open space or lane that is part of the pedestrian area will be adequate. Meetings with local police and fire companies will help determine these functional requirements. For example, in Ithaca, New York, the fire department built a model of the mall to study access

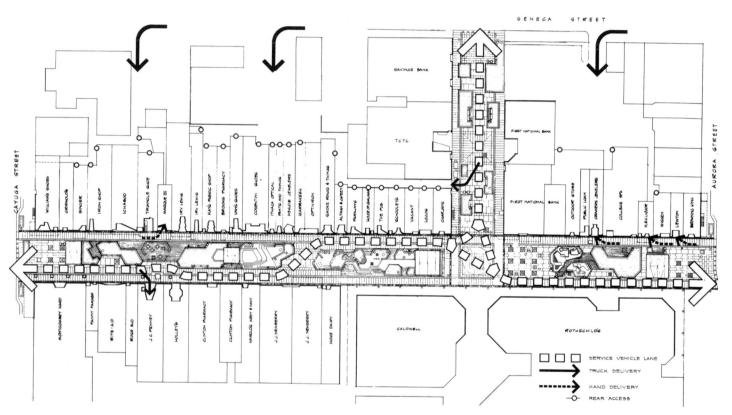

Service access study, Ithaca Commons. (Photograph courtesy of Anton J. Egner and Associates.)

for fire-fighting vehicles and equipment suitability.

Pedestrian Circulation

The primary objectives of improved pedestrian circulation are safety, security, convenience, continuity, coherence, comfort, and aesthetics. Fulfilling one of these objectives generally increases the opportunities for meeting or improving the others. Ease of pedestrian circulation with safety from vehicular conflict is one of the primary purposes

and benefits of developing central city malls.

Two methods of reducing conflicts between pedestrians and vehicles are time separation and space separation. Traffic signals are a mechanism for providing time separation. There are still conflicts, however, because of vehicular turning movements. In some cities an "all walk" sequence where pedestrians have exclusive crossing rights is used at busy downtown intersections. This system generally

produces greater numbers of people waiting at corners to cross the street than would otherwise be the case.

Space separation is achieved by closing streets to vehicles and creating malls. The full mall acts as a pedestrian plaza, and people may walk freely between the two sides of the space. Space separation can also be achieved by the use of underpasses or overpasses; if these are not within the direct line of pedestrian traffic, however, they

A service lane is used in Penn Square, Reading, Pennslyvania.

may not be fully used because of the inconvenience of a longer walking distance. This has happened on the Fort Street Mall in Honolulu, Hawaii (see p. 102).

The inventory of the proposed mall area should include the dimensions of each street and sidewalk. Also included should be information on all traffic regulations, signs, signal locations, signal cycle length, and traffic (volumes from the traffic survey). The sidewalk survey should show the locations and dimensions of buildings and the transit system locations or entrances.

The inventory should also examine pedestrian trips, including their origins and destinations, purposes, time of day, and volume. For large pedestrian networks this information is difficult to obtain, and special methods must be used. These methods include cordon counts, origin and destination surveys, pedestrian density surveys by aerial photographs, and mathematical modeling.

Trip Purpose and Characteristics

Most pedestrian trips are relatively short, only a few blocks, because pedestrians seek parking spaces within 600 feet of their destinations. If the purposes and types of pedestrian trips are understood, better pedestrian facilities can be developed. Pedestrian trip purpose is closely related to the type of land use associated with trip origin or destination. The number of trips attracted or generated by an activity

Space separation is achieved by the use of an underpass at Vallingby, Sweden.

depends on its size and type. For example, large retail stores will attract more trips than small retail stores.

Pedestrian trips are categorized into three major types: (1) terminal trips, (2) functional trips, and (3) recreational trips.

TERMINAL TRIPS are made to and from home or points associated with transportation mode areas: parking lots, bus stops, and transportation stations. FUNCTIONAL TRIPS are made to carry out a specific function, such as business trips related to work or personal business trips involving shopping, dining, or going to a doctor's office. RECREATIONAL TRIPS are made for purposes related to leisure time. These include going to the theatre, concerts, and sporting events, as well as social activities in which walking is one of the primary purposes.

NODES In the pedestrian network there are two basic types of nodes. One is the origin and destination (node) of the walking trip. Nodes are centers of pedestrian activity or points of concentration.

These are classified as primary or terminal nodes and secondary or activity nodes.

PRIMARY NODES are associated with mode transfer where walking trips begin and end, such as parking areas and transit stops.

SECONDARY NODES are other locations that attract trips from primary nodes as well as from other secondary nodes, such as offices, stores, and restaurants.

In summary, various types of studies must be carried out to determine whether there are problems related to pedestrian circulation in a given area. For example, the analysis may show that large numbers of pedestrians use the particular area designated for a mall, and that certain sidewalk areas must be significantly widened to accommodate the pedestrian traffic. The study may also demonstrate that space separation is needed to solve problems of pedestrian/vehicular conflict. This is an important consideration in determining the overall feasibility of the mall and its type—whether it should be a full, a semi, or a transit mall.

Utilities

In considering mall development, it is necessary to review the existing utilities and to plan for upgrading the systems when necessary. These utilities include storm water drainage, sewage disposal, electricity, gas, steam, potable water, and telephone. If a street has outdated utility lines, such as combined sanitary and storm water systems, the lines should be separated while the block or blocks are being reconstructed. A new utility core through the entire block may be desirable. If electric lines to existing light poles are still above ground, it may be possible to place new lines below grade.

The costs for revamping the utility system must be carefully evaluated because a major share of the project cost may be absorbed by these lines, which are invisible on the surface. In some malls the utilities have cost as much as one third to two thirds of the total construction budget. (See Table 2-1.)

TABLE 2-1

Utility Costs versus Total Costs

Location	Mall Name	Construction Cost (dollars)	Utility Cost as Percent of Construction Cost
Fresno, California	Fulton Mall	1,600,000	62.5
Napa, California	Parkway Mall	1,500,000	30
Oxnard, California	Park Plaza Mall	653,000	30
New London, Connecticut	Captain's Walk	1,426,000	21
Toccoa, Georgia	Downtown Shopping Mall	1,800,000	25
Atchison, Kansas	Downtown Mall	3,600,000	14
Parsons, Kansas	Parsons Plaza	850,000	12
Baltimore, Maryland	Lexington Street Mall	800,000	65
Baltimore, Maryland	Oldtown Mall	2,600,000	33
Battle Creek, Michigan	Michigan Mall	2,000,000	10
Lansing, Michigan	Washington Square Mall	850,000	47
Minneapolis, Minnesota	Nicollet Mall	3,800,000	66
Helena, Montana	Last Chance Mall	417,000	33
Painesville, Ohio	Main Street Mall	143,000	63
Portland, Oregon	Portland Transit Mall	15,000,000	13
Erie, Pennsylvania	Downtown Mall	1,400,000	21
Pittsburgh, Pennsylvania	East Liberty Mall	3,585,000	40
Reading, Pennsylvania	Penn Square	1,600,000	33
Tacoma, Washington	Broadway Street Plaza	1,500,000	12

Even if existing utilities are in good condition, their locations must be carefully considered so that the lines can be maintained when necessary with as little disruption as possible to mall activities.

A very detailed topographic survey is needed, locating all of the existing facilities and giving rim and invert elevations of manholes and catch basins, as well as elevations at the entrances to all buildings and at intersections, service roads, and any other critical places. The city engineer can provide information on sizes of lines. This information should be verified by the utility companies. Perhaps these companies have planned to upgrade their lines and would be willing to do the work in conjunction with the development of the mall.

Older cities often have some anti-quated systems, such as steam lines for heating parts of a downtown area, or perhaps combined sanitary and storm lines. These lines may need work because of their age. The mall development provides an opportunity to separate the storm water lines from the sanitary lines, to build vaults so that the lines may be easily serviced in the future, or to do other needed work. In any case the utility systems must be carefully reviewed, along with the soils beneath the mall.

Existing Buildings

Existing buildings in the area of the proposed mall must be carefully

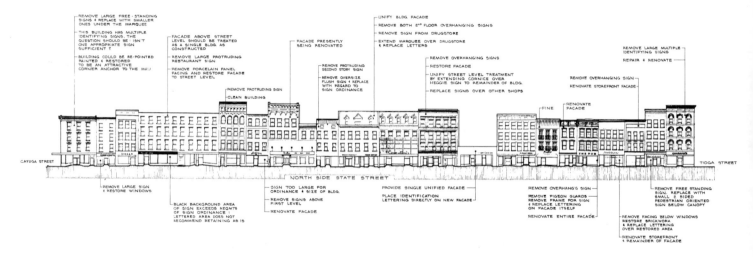

Existing building survey, Ithaca Commons. (Photograph courtesy of Anton J. Egner and Associates.)

surveyed as to their condition, height, front footage, and architectural character. Architectural character includes the building facade, color, texture, materials, window type, and roof style.

Some of these buildings may have basement vaults that project beneath existing sidewalks. The size, location, and structural condition of each vault must be determined. How much room is there between existing vaults and the finished grade of the existing sidewalks? Will the vaults have to be waterproofed if new sidewalks are installed? Also, will the vaults be able to bear additional weight if necessary, or must they be rebuilt?

If a particular building is in bad condition, costs would be incurred by having it torn down in order to build the mall. Programs may sometimes be developed concurrently with the mall construction to help merchants finance new facades or carry out other rehabilitation or renovation of their buildings. This has been done for several malls, such as Oldtown Mall in Baltimore (see p. 144).

Reviewing these factors for several different vicinities that have some potential for a downtown mall may show the condition of buildings in a particular area to be a significant factor.

Street Furnishings

Elements on existing sidewalks or overhanging sidewalks are called street furnishings. These include

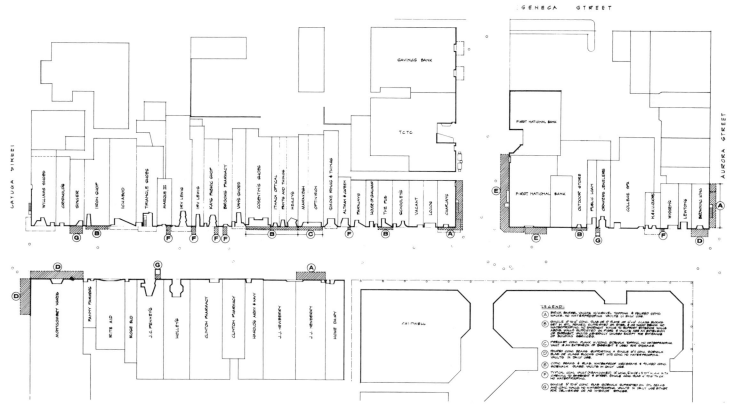

Vault plan, Ithaca Commons. (Photograph courtesy of Anton J. Egner and Associates.)

signs, lights, traffic signals, parking meters, fire hydrants, benches, and flower pots.

These elements must be inventoried in the overall street context. A new sign ordinance may be necessary to improve the aesthetics of the downtown. Elements such as fire hydrants or light poles may have to be relocated if a mall is developed. Traffic signals of the older type, hanging across streets by overhead wires, should be replaced by new modular units that include the traffic signals, pedestrian walk signals, and night lighting.

Maintenance

Once a mall has been constructed, it must be maintained. Maintenance consists of sweeping the mall, removing trash, replacing light bulbs, removing snow in many regions, and watering, spraying, and fertilizing trees and shrubs, as well as replacing broken items and perhaps planting flowers in the spring and putting up Christmas decorations in the fall. Can the proposed mall be designed so that it can be well maintained at a reasonable cost? Durable materials and good detailing and construction methods help keep maintenance costs down.

Continuous maintenance will be necessary and must be programmed into the overall cost of the mall. Who will carry out the maintenance? In many areas, cities will take care of this function. Often, however, supplemental maintenance is necessary. If state law permits assessment of property owners for this purpose, the problem may be solved; if not, an association to manage this service must be formed.

NATURAL FACTORS

Natural factors such as the climate, topography, soils, water table, and vegetation of a proposed area must also be reviewed.

Climate

Temperature, humidity, precipitation, and wind are important considerations in the design of a mall. If the mall is located in an area with severe climate—either hot or cold, or involving much precipitation—covered walkways may be desirable. This type of feature can be quite expensive, but it has been used in the design of several malls. Microclimate or variation in local climate will also have an important impact on the location of elements within a mall. Shade trees, for example, could be planted in the areas of the mall having the most exposure to the sun. Since people enjoy sitting in shaded areas that provide protection from the sun,

This canopy provides some weather protection in Wilkes-Barre, Pennsylvania, by Bohlin and Powell.

CENTRAL CITY MALLS

benches might be added in these areas. If a fountain is a feature of the mall, having the sunlight reflect off the water would be an important consideration in its location. Climate is also important in the design of construction details and in the maintenance of a mall. In cold climates, footings for various elements must be below the frost level. Also, consideration must be given to the types of paving materials used in the construction of the mall. Will the use of salt during winter months have a detrimental effect on paving materials or planted areas? These factors are very important in the design of the mall.

Soils and Water Table
Soils must be studied to see whether there is any limitation on the type of facilities to be placed on the mall. In addition, the soil study will consider placement of utility lines and foundations. The water table must also be explored in relation to subsurface conditions. In areas with special situations, such as a city with old mine shafts beneath it, special consultants may be necessary to review possible problems.

Topography
The topography of an area often has a great influence on the location and design of a mall. The topography will also influence the location of activity areas. In some malls topography has been used to create unique effects.

The topography of the existing area

Topography has been used to an advantage at Essex Mall, Salem, Massachusetts, by Collins, DuTot Partnership.

must be studied very carefully, and a comprehensive topographic survey must be carried out so that all critical elevations on a block may be reviewed when the mall is in the design stage. This review should point out problems related to dealing with water runoff, saving existing trees, and meeting grades at entrances to buildings.

Vegetation

What types of trees, if any, exist where the proposed mall is to be built? Will planting trees in a particular block encounter any problems, such as vaults located under the present sidewalks? The uses of vegetation are discussed in Chapter 5.

SOCIOECONOMIC FACTORS

A study of the community and its social and economic structure is important in determining the feasibility of a mall.

Business in the downtown area must be of sufficient regional potential to justify the cost of a mall. The level of business should be projected to increase or at least hold the line. If this is not the case, the feasibility of the mall is in doubt.

The size and costs of the mall must be realistic in relation to the volume of business taking place on it or adjacent to it, and also in relation to the property values on or near it.

Market Analysis

Socioeconomic feasibility is based on a market analysis and projection. The analysis should be carried out by experienced professionals and should cover the trade area, population characteristics, buying power, and competition.

TRADE AREA The trade area is the region that supplies major continuing patronage for a business

area. It includes the primary trade area, within a 5-minute drive or a radius of about 1.5 miles; the secondary trade area, within a 15- to 20-minute drive or 3- to 5-mile radius; and the tertiary trade area, within a 25-minute drive or 7- to 8-mile radius. The survey of the trade area should consider traffic modes, access to the mall, and location of competitive facilities.

POPULATION The population characteristics within the trade area must be studied to identify the potential user of the mall. These characteristics include population number, population growth, and factors such as income level, age, and family size. This information is obtained from census data.

SOCIAL CONCERNS Other social factors to be identified, in addition to who the user or urban consumer is, are the activities, events, and programs that he or she desires to be programmed into the design and operation of a mall. Downtown areas are busy places providing a variety of activities, features, and functions. These elements, properly located, will help to generate an improved social environment in the downtown, which in turn will lead to improved economic patterns.

Public opinion surveys can establish what new activities, uses, and features would be desirable in a mall. Objectives can then be established for space requirements for these elements when the mall is designed. Promotional events such as puppet shows, car shows, boat shows, fashion shows, parades, art exhibits, craft exhibits, fund raising events, and special programs such as band concerts can be held. Other uses relate to vendors, outdoor restaurants, information booths, or related items which add to the particular sense of a place. Feature elements include items such as fountains, sculpture, children's play-

grounds, and clock towers.

Upon completion of the mall, promotion should be actively started to attract people. The promotion can be aimed at increased pedestrian traffic, tourists, young people, senior citizens, and families. An ongoing promotion coordinator may be hired to schedule a wide variety of events to help create interest in the mall and draw people to it.

PURCHASING POWER Income levels within the trade area are important in showing the number of dollars available in relation to expenditures for categories of goods and services such as food, general merchandise, apparel, furniture, automobile parts, gasoline, and drugs. This information is available from the U.S. Bureau of the Census.

Economic specialists can estimate expenditures from various parts of the trade area. Personal income trends and projections may also be made to determine potential sales.

COMPETITION An important step in the analysis is to study existing retail facilities in the overall trade area to determine how much retail sales may increase with the development of the new mall. This study will review facilities in the central business district, suburban shopping facilities, and potential future facilities.

Cost/Benefit

When a mall is developed, insufficient spending may limit attainment of the proposed objectives. On the other hand, high construction costs in relation to benefits may not be justified. Therefore the proper balance must be found.

The cost/benefit approach enables the potential economic benefits, as well as the functional, environmental, and social or community benefits, to be projected and evaluated.

Projected goals and objectives

should be formulated so that benefits can be measured. Economic benefits can be projected from the market analysis data. Enough data are generally available to determine factors such as projected increase in retail sales, tax revenue, and property taxes, increase in the market value of improvements, and increase in the number of jobs. Other potential benefits are higher land values, greater numbers of customers, and heavier use of public transit.

Social and community benefits may be evaluated by means of opinion surveys with such questions as, "Will the mall help to upgrade existing community facilities, provide for new ones, or increase open space?" Functional benefits include such things as improving downtown traffic, service, safety, and security. Some examples of environmental benefits are control of air pollution, improvement of aesthetic quality, and preservation of historic buildings.

A cost/benefit analysis can bring many favorable factors to the public's attention and be instrumental in arousing community support for building a mall.

POLITICAL, FUNDING, AND LEGAL FACTORS

A feasibility study is more than a review of traffic, parking, and market analysis; it is a public relations document. It must be a sound document competently done by professionals so that it can be used as a selling tool.

Political Factors

An important question is whether a mall is politically feasible. Can the votes and approvals needed to make the mall a reality be obtained? Who has the final decision-making power on closing a street—the mayor, city council, or state? Those who advocate building a mall should find out which groups or individuals may present problems and then meet with them to discuss the benefits of the mall and at least to neutralize their doubts so that they will not hinder the project. The feasibility study should help answer all the questions that may arise about the mall and should be made available to the public. Parts of the study may be published in the local newspapers, and copies placed in the library.

Obtaining an early commitment to the project and support from the business community, property owners, newspapers, politicians, and municipal administrators is helpful, as is establishing a downtown study committee with representatives from all the above groups to keep the project moving and to act as spokesmen for it.

Funding

If the feasibility analysis demonstrates that the project is viable, funding can be obtained. Funding from as many sources as possible is desirable, so that each can make a contribution to the overall project.

Several types of funding are available for malls. The federal government gives Community Development Program grants to many cities.

A portion of these funds may be allotted to a mall.

The Department of Commerce, Economic Development Administration, is another possible source of funds. It makes money available to provide jobs in project areas under its Public Works Program. The Urban Mass Transportation Administration also makes grants for projects related to a coordinated transportation system. This agency has funded projects such as the Chestnut Street Transitway in Philadelphia and the Portland Transit Mall.

Funding by state community affairs departments is also possible in some areas. The Hamilton Mall in Allentown, Pennsylvania, was partially funded in this way. Sometimes special assessment districts are established. Many states have legislation that permits assessment on properties abutting or adjoining a mall. All commercial and retail establishments should be included in the districts. Contributions to the development should be mandatory rather than voluntary. The assessment district may be based on front footage or gross square footage. A percentage of construction cost and maintenance can be financed by this method. Cities issue bonds, and properties in the assessment district pay off the interest and principal. Assessments can also be used to match funds from outside sources.

Legal Factors

State law must be researched to see what is possible under the laws on assessment. If legislation does not exist on assessment, a bill can be introduced into the state legislature. The state highway department can advise whether there are legal problems in closing or changing a city street that is also a state route.

In most cities an ordinance must be passed by the city council and the mayor in order to narrow an existing city street or to close a street completely to create a full mall. In some cases a bill may have to be enacted by a state legislature in order to establish a mall.

In the state of Washington, the Edmonds City Council resolved to have a pedestrian mall and then found that it was legally impossible. Through the Association of Washington Cities, Edmonds avoided litigation when the state legislature approved a bill to create a mall.

3 Context and Form Characteristics

As a mall is developed, it should be viewed in the context of the entire downtown. This means that, in studying the physical relationships of a mall to the central city and in strengthening the mall's identity or image, one must go beyond the immediate environment of the mall and examine the larger central city context.

(*Preceding pages*)
Aerial view of downtown Portland, Oregon. (Photograph courtesy of Tri-Met.)

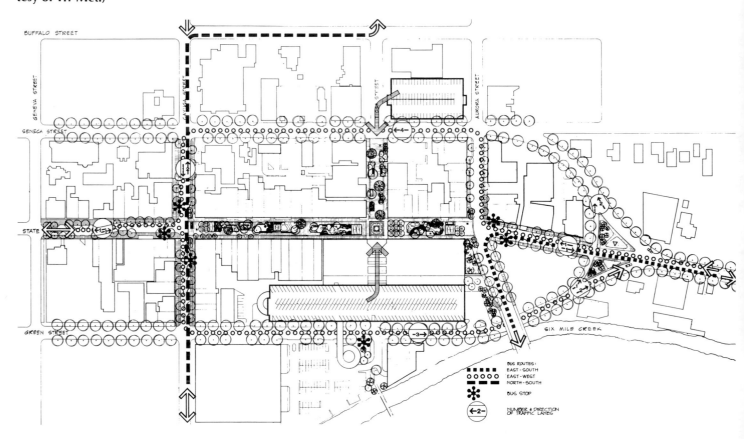

Overall context of Ithaca Commons, with study of bus routes. (Photograph courtesy of Anton J. Egner and Associates.)

CENTRAL CITY MALLS

CONTEXT

Central City Image

The image of a central city is based on its shape, color, texture, arrangement, and sensory quality, all of which give the observer clues to its identity and structure.

Image has been classified into five elements which may be isolated for closer study. These elements are paths, nodes, edges, districts, and landmarks. They are described as follows.

Paths

Paths are the circulation routes or lines along which people move. They are the streets, walks, and transit and rail lines.

Nodes

Nodes are centers of activity into which one can enter. They are junctions or crossings of paths, or points of concentration such as plazas. They may also be places of transportation mode activity such as railroad, bus, or subway stations.

Edges

Edges are linear boundaries that distinguish one area or region from another. An edge may be a river (see p. 26), which is a strong feature in outlining the boundary of a city, or it may be a path such as an elevated roadway, or a row of buildings forming the outline for an area.

Districts

Districts are medium to large parts of a city that have common distinguishing characteristics. They are identifiable from the inside and can

Market Street in San Francisco is a path with several systems of circulation, including pedestrian walks, buses, subways, and automobiles.

This node is the subway station in downtown Stockholm, Sweden.

be used for exterior reference if viewed from the outside. The more easily they can be seen from a distance, the more useful they are in guiding direction. A district is an area of a city with which people identify and which generally has a name, such as North Side, East End, or Hill Section.

Landmarks

A landmark is a physical object such as a building, tower, sign, dome, mountain, or hill. Landmarks may vary in scale, may be close or distant, and sometimes may be seen only from specific approaches, as from the junction along a path. Landmarks aid in the identification of points of choice and direction. A landmark may be a place known to an observer which gives him cues so that he may make a choice, for example, as to which turn in a road junction to take. Distant landmarks also aid in maintaining direction. Paths, nodes, edges, and landmarks work in conjunction with each other to form the structure of the central city. Of these elements, paths are the most important in providing order. Major paths should have their own identities. Each should have some quality that distinguishes it from the surrounding network. This can be spatial quality, a special paving pattern, a unique texture of material on walks or building facades, or a particular lighting pattern, planting design, or activity that gives continuity to the path.

The Charles River, Cambridge, Massachusetts, forms a strong linear edge.

The Town Hall and Mangia Tower, seen from the Piazza del Campo, Siena, Italy, form a dramatic landmark. The tower, which rises to a height of 334.5 feet (102 meters), was built in 1338–1348.

In any existing central city area where a mall may be built, there is an image even if it is cluttered and not apparent. In developing a mall the challenge lies in reshaping an existing street environment and strengthening its image. A mall can therefore enhance the image of the central city by helping to clarify its structure and identity.

Inventory and Analysis

An inventory and analysis must be made of existing physical elements in the vicinity of the mall. Strong features must be identified and reinforced, while weak elements are removed or strengthened. For example, a city may have unsightly overhead wiring for its street lighting. These wires should be placed underground.

Perhaps a particular building is run-down and needs to be rehabilitated. Graphic maps, drawings, and/or diagrams should be made to illustrate these factors or conditions. In an inventory of central city fea-tures related to the mall's image, items of visual pollution become evident. In many older cities there is a clutter of street furnishings, such as traffic signals, poles, signs, and parking meters.

The analysis of physical factors can also reveal which, if any, street furnishings are causing visual pollu-tion. At the urban scale the details of elements in the street may be as important as buildings in determin-ing the aesthetic quality of a city. It is therefore most important to

Clutter of overhead wiring.

CENTRAL CITY MALLS

review the elements that provide form for the city, identifying the items that give continuity to the downtown context and restructuring other items to improve visual quality. The following discussion reviews the form characteristics that provide design quality. This should lead to improved understanding of the design factors and form characteristics with which architects and landscape architects must be familiar in order to relate a mall to an existing urban context.

FORM CHARACTERISTICS

The following characteristics should be considered in giving design or aesthetic quality to urban space.

Figure-Ground

Figure-ground is the contrast of an object to the ground. An element appears as a figure if it stands out against undisturbed ground. For example, trees are the figures that stand out against the sky acting as ground. Other vertical elements on a mall, such as lights, can stand out as figures in contrast to buildings. Such contrast gives an object clarity and identity.

Continuity

Continuity is provided by a series of coherent parts. The parts may be related by keeping a common scale, form, texture, or color for a space or area. For example, use of brick pavers of a particular color on a mall gives continuity to the paving.

This Milles sculpture in Stockholm, Sweden, stands out as a figure against the sky acting as ground.

Continuity of paving can be achieved by the use of a paving material such as brick or concrete.

Sequence

Sequence is continuity in the perception of space or objects arranged to provide a succession of visual change. It may create motion or mood, or give direction. One space in a sequence may create mood by having a bosque of trees or an overhead structure to provide enclosure, while the following space is open.

Repetition

Repetition is the simplest kind of sequence. It may involve shape, color, or texture, and only a single part need be repeated. For example, a particular type of street light could be selected and repeated throughout a mall area or the overall central city.

Rhythm

Rhythm is a sequence of repetitive elements interrupted at specific intervals. Rhythm can be incorporated into a paving pattern by creating a design with a change from brick to concrete bands at specific intervals.

Size and Scale

The size of an object or space is relative and depends on the distance of the object from the observer. Scale denotes relative size and is based on the height of an average observer, 5 feet 9 inches. The scale of space, therefore, is related to the observer himself. In viewing a building, the eye has an angle of vision of about 27 degrees. To see a whole building at this angle, one must be at a distance that equals twice the building height.

(*Opposite page*)
Oldtown Mall, Baltimore, generally has a narrow street width of 45 feet and, with abutting buildings of two to four stories, has an interesting scale. (Photograph courtesy of O'Malley and Associates, Inc.)

A sequence of space can be provided by moving from an open space to a space with a feeling of enclosure.

Repetition is achieved by the use of bollards with built-in lighting, and rhythm by alternating brick with concrete bands in the paving, at Penn Square, Reading, Pennsylvania, by the Delta Group.

In relating outdoor space to buildings there is a sense of balance when a space has a width equal to the height of the building or twice the building height. Once the space is larger than four times the height of the building, interaction between building and space dissipates.

In a space 80 × 80 feet in size, people can still identify each other. As spaces go beyond about 150 × 200 feet in size, it is difficult to retain the feeling of intimacy of smaller spaces.

Shape

Shape gives quality to the relative form of an object. What is the shape or form of a space? Is it rectilinear, curvilinear, or triangular? (See p. 30.)

Proportion

Proportion is the ratio of height to width to length. Ratios have been developed to achieve a series of dimensions that are related to each other and to a largest size. The Greeks built their temples with a length/width ratio of 1.618 : 1. Simple ratios such as 1 : 1, 1 : 2, 2 : 3, 3 : 4, and 3 : 5 are perceived and used to design architectural elements.

Hierarchy

Hierarchy is a system used to rank sizes or colors. Hierarchy can be applied to rank the sizes of elements in a paving pattern or to give prominence to an area around a sculpture or fountain by changing the size or color of the paving materials.

CONTEXT AND FORM CHARACTERISTICS

Dominance

Dominance denotes importance over other parts because of having the largest size or the most prominent position. In a mall there may be a dominant space or area containing a special activity or focal element.

Texture and Pattern

When one cannot determine the size and shape of individual parts as they form a continuous surface, there is texture. When one can dif- ferentiate the parts forming a whole, there is a pattern. Texture can be provided by the type of materials used or by surface treatment of elements such as walks made of aggregate concrete. Pattern is important in walk designs for adding color, contrast, and interest.

Transparency

Transparency gives depth by over- laps or penetration of vision. Transparency can occur in paving patterns where elements overlap and changes in color make the pattern more interesting.

Direction

Direction is a line along which things lie or a reference toward a point or area that gives order to ele- ments. For example, compass direc- tion is often used to orient the system of street layout in a city into north-south and east-west.

Similarity

Similarity occurs when like elements

Space in rectilinear format at Constitu- tion Plaza, Hartford, Connecticut. (Photograph courtesy of Sasaki Associates.)

form groups. Repetition, color, shape, size, and texture contribute to this characteristic.

Volumes and Enclosure
To achieve clearly defined spaces, we must consider space-forming elements and the volumes contained, such as the base plane, overhead plane, and vertical plane.

BASE PLANES Base planes relate all objects on a horizontal surface.

VERTICAL PLANES Vertical planes have an important function in articulating the uses of spaces. Buildings are usually the most important vertical elements in forming spaces. They also act as points of reference or landmarks.

OVERHEAD PLANES Overhead planes are important in giving definition to the height of a space.

Motion
Motion is a process of moving or changing time or position. It reinforces direction or distance and can give a sense of form in motion. As an observer walks along a mall, his point of reference or angle of vision of objects changes. This provides a variety of views and sunlight and shadow patterns, depending on the time of day and season of the year.

Time
Continuity over a period of time, or the sequential relationship that any event has to any other, past, present, or future, is important. For example, as new buildings are added to an urban area they can be

A canopy system used in Wilkes-Barre, Pennsylvania, by Bohlin and Powell.

Transparency is created by overlapping paving elements.

related to older structures by the use of materials, proportion of architectural elements, texture, and color. Preserving old structures in a city and adding or infilling with new structures provides continuity with our past heritage.

Sensory Quality

The sense of a place—its visual impression, and its appeal to one's senses of sound, smell, and touch— adds a further dimension to the design of urban spaces. Do people relate to or feel at ease in a particular place? Features that please the senses can give a mall an atmosphere which attracts people. Fountains, sculpture, shaded areas in which to sit and view other people, and appealing activities all help create this environment.

Cafe in River City Mall, Louisville, Kentucky. (Photograph courtesy of Johnson, Johnson, and Roy, Inc.)

The Lexington
Street Mall in Balti-
more is inviting
with its canopy of
trees and raised
planters. (Photo-
graph courtesy of
O'Malley and
Associates, Inc.)

4
Design Elements and Street Furniture

Designing and choosing furnishings for a mall should be approached in the context of both the comprehensive urban environment of the mall and the specific streets where the furnishings are to be used. Furnishings are often selected from catalogues without sufficient data on performance. This practice can perpetuate the visual disorder that we wish to eliminate.

The design of a mall must consider the type, size, scale, location, and materials of all street furnishings.

These elements include paving, lighting, graphic design, sculpture, fountains, bollards, seating, planters, telephones, kiosks, shelters, and canopies.

The design, detailing, and choice of materials of the furnishings are important not only for design continuity but also for both durability and ease of maintenance. Appropriate detailing and use of materials in the urban landscape are therefore of primary importance to the success of a mall. Experienced

(*Preceding pages*) **Oldtown Mall, Baltimore, Maryland. (Photograph courtesy of O'Malley and Associates, Inc.)**

This clock tower, located on Nicollet Mall, Minneapolis, is 21 feet high with a face 4 feet square. The lower portion of the clock has an animated sculpture. (Photograph courtesy of the Downtown Council of Minneapolis.)

urban designers and landscape architects should be involved in the design and coordination of this phase of the mall development.

PAVING

Scale, pattern, color, and texture are form characteristics related to the design of the city floor or paving concept for a mall. The paving pattern gives order to the overall design of a mall. It also provides a sense of scale by the use of materials such as brick, concrete, and stone. The slope of the paving and the way in which water runoff is handled are also important items that should be considered.

Pavers

Pavers may be set on concrete or bituminous bases or placed on 2 inches of sand above a crushed stone base.

CONCRETE Concrete pavers are made in many shapes, sizes, and textures. Some newer types are available in a 3-inch thickness, look like brick, and have interlocking shapes for added stability. This material may be placed on sand above a crushed stone base and is strong enough for automobile or bus traffic when used for a semimall or transit mall.

Concrete may also be poured in place. A variety of textures are available with this material. Poured concrete may also be used with brick pavers, textured or aggregate concrete pavers, or stone pavers to form paving patterns.

Concrete Z-brick pavers are used on the Lower Main Street Mall, Paterson, New Jersey.

Smooth concrete bands with aggregate infill provide an interesting textured effect for walk areas.

BRICK Brick, the oldest artificial material, offers a durable, long lasting surface requiring little maintenance. Brick offers a great variety of textures and colors, is available in many sizes and shapes, and provides a hard surface resistant to wear and cracking. Pavers for walks are often 4 × 8 × 1 inch and may be arranged in many different patterns.

STONE Stone, one of the oldest paving materials, offers a long lasting surface needing little maintenance. Granite is one of the most durable of stones and is often used in urban areas. For added interest it can be used as granite sets, which have a good texture, for paving minor circulation areas such as those used for seating, berms, and areas around trees, fountains, or sculptures.

ASPHALT Asphalt may be used in the form of pavers or dumped in place. Although asphalt does not have the variety of textures of concrete, it provides a softer walking surface. Asphalt pavers come in a variety of shapes, such as hexagonals, and offer a choice of colors and aggregates.

The color of the material is an important aesthetic factor in the paving design. Color adds interest, particularly in areas with limited amounts of sunshine. Some colors will be compatible with materials used on buildings along the mall or may contrast with these buildings to provide interest. In areas with much sunshine, light-colored materials

Brick pavers laid in running bond are usually set on a concrete slab with 3/8-inch mortar joints or on a bituminous base with tight joints.

Hexagonal brick pavers form an interesting and durable surface.

Brick and concrete are often used to form paving patterns, as at Essex Mall, Salem, Massachusetts, by the Collins, DuTot Partnership.

such as natural concrete tend to reflect much light, which is uncomfortable to the pedestrian's vision. This factor must therefore be considered in the choice of materials in the design concept.

Durability and Ease of Maintenance

Durability and ease of maintenance are important factors in selecting paving materials. Low cost of initial installation may not be as important in the long run as low maintenance costs. In areas where snow removal is a consideration, materials resistant to salt or other snow melting chemicals should be reviewed. The provision of underground snow melting equipment may also be a consideration in the design of the mall.

TREE GRATES

Tree grates may become part of the paving pattern of a mall. When trees are planted directly in the base plane of a mall, the grates become an integral design element in the paving pattern.

Tree grates are used to give a wider expanse to walk areas, to allow air and water to reach the roots of a tree, and to limit maintenance of the open areas around trees in paved areas (see page 42). Tree

Granite sets give color and texture to special types of areas such as the crosswalks at Essex Mall, Salem, Massachusetts.

Tree grates form part of the paving pattern on the Hamilton Mall, Allentown, Pennsylvania.

Asphalt pavers are used in similar ways to concrete and are good for walk areas. Because of their dark color, they also reduce glare from reflected sunlight.

grates also add interest in scale, pattern, color, and texture to the urban environment.

LIGHTING

Night lighting extends the time for participation in activities on the mall. It provides safety and security and adds interest by accenting plantings, fountains, sculpture, buildings, graphics, and other features in the urban context.
Night lighting for malls is often designed by architects and landscape architects working in conjunction with electrical engineers.

Illumination

For comfort and a feeling of security, one must have adequate light to illuminate details and to make objects brighter than the sky. Unless an observer is looking directly at a light source, he sees only light reflected by surfaces around him. What he actually sees is the brightness of light. If brightness is excessive, it becomes glare. Glare interferes with vision and causes loss of contrast between detail and background.

OUTPUT AND MEASUREMENT
To measure the luminous output of lamps, a unit for the light producing power of a light source was established. It is called a lumen and is defined as the rate at which light falls on a 1-square-foot surface area, all parts of which are 1 foot from a surface with the intensity of one candle.

Illumination on a surface is measured in footcandles. A footcandle is defined as the illumination on 1 square foot over which 1 lumen is evenly distributed. This means that 1 footcandle equals 1 lumen per square foot.

The footcandle is the unit used in calculating lighting installations.

LIGHT SOURCES Several types of light sources are available for night lighting. They are incandescent, fluorescent, and high intensity discharge lamps such as mercury, metal halide, and high pressure sodium.

INCANDESCENT light has a warm, reddish color. Objects are accentuated when this light is used, and texture is distinguishable. With a typical 100-watt A-19 bulb, lamp life is 750 hours with a 1750-lumen output. Extended service bulbs are available which last 2500 to 8000 hours but have a somewhat lower lumen output.

Another type of incandescent light called a quartz line is often used for spotlights or floodlights. These bulbs have about a 2000-hour lamp life and, at 100 watts, produce 1900 lumens.

Although the initial cost of incandescent fixtures is less by $50 to $75 than that of mercury lamps, the operating cost is higher.

Because of its warm color, incandescent light is best on yellow, red, and brown objects and is very

Sometimes special openings for the night lighting of trees are combined into the design of the grates, as at Crocker Plaza, San Francisco, by Sasaki, Walker Associates, Inc.

desirable in pedestrian areas where warm color is important.

FLUORESCENT lamps produce a dull, flat light with dark objects viewed in silhouette. Fluourescent bulbs come in bluish, yellowish, or pinkish colors. A 100-watt fluorescent bulb has a lamp life of 12,000 to 18,000 hours and produces about 6300 lumens. Cool white lamps produce a neutral to moderately cool effect with good color acceptance.

Fluorescent lamps have increased efficiency over incandescent lamps, but lamp efficiency varies with cold temperature conditions unless a cold weather ballast and enclosed fixture are used. Fluorescent lighting also has a higher initial cost than incandescent.

MERCURY VAPOR has a sparkling quality. It gives two and a half times more light than do incandescent fixtures for the power used. A 100-watt mercury bulb has a lamp life of 24,000 hours with an output of 4200 lumens. Mercury also maintains a high output of lumens over its lamp life. Clear mercury lamps have a cool, greenish color and are good for lighting green objects such as plants.

Deluxe mercury lamps have been improved in color with red, yellow, and blue strengthened. These lamps have good color acceptance and are often used to light pedestrian or street areas.

METAL HALIDE is similar to mercury. It is very efficient, giving about an 8000-lumen output at 100 watts with a 10,000-hour life.

HIGH PRESSURE SODIUM offers small lamp size and good light control. It has a very high efficiency and, for 100 watts, gives about a 9500-lumen output with a 12,000-hour life. It provides a warm, yellowish light and is used for street lighting.

STREET LIGHTING Although some cities have lighting levels of from 10 to 20 footcandles in core areas, many cities have lower levels. The Illuminating Engineering Society calls for a minimum of 1.2 footcandles on collector streets in commercial areas. At signalized intersections, there should be lighting with at least three times the intensity of street lighting.

In lighting city areas, glare can be a problem if high intensity lights less than 35 feet in height are used. If lower lights are used, cut-off shields often help to minimize glare.

MALL LIGHTING Light standards in relation to pedestrian scale generally have a maximum height of 12 feet. Where steps are present, care should be taken to provide adequate light to illuminate these areas.

For comfort in viewing lights with clear acrylic globes, it is best to use no more than a 75-watt mercury bulb with a refractor over it. There are also fixtures that reflect light downward without the need for seeing the light source. These lights,

Mall lighting at 12-foot height at Gallery Place, Washington, D.C., by Arrowstreet, Inc.

while giving good illumination, are generally easier on the eyes of the viewer. Several of these fixtures use either 100- or 175-watt mercury bulbs. They also come in a wide range of shapes such as cubes or form circular or rectangular volumes.

GRAPHIC DESIGN

Signs

A comprehensive system of signs is needed for central city areas and for a mall. Signs are part of the overall graphic design for a city. They convey messages that are essential to the function, safety, and security of a mall.

In general, signs conveying the same information in the central city area should be consistent in color, shape, message, and location. They should be easily recognizable in the urban context. Signs must also relate to the varying modes of circulation. Different systems are needed for pedestrians and for motorists. Signs should, for example, prepare a driver in advance for turning decisions or for various road conditions. There are four basic purposes for which signs are needed: to provide mall identity, to improve traffic flow, to identify commercial facilities, and to provide information on the direction or location of activities.

Reflected light is provided by these fixtures.

In the Chestnut Street Transitway, Philadelphia, clusters of eight smoky gray Plexiglas, acrylic plastic globes are used. (Photograph courtesy of Rohm and Haas Company.)

MALL IDENTITY A symbol or logo can be very important in giving identity to a mall. The logo can also be useful for public relations purposes.

TRAFFIC SIGNS Traffic signs include a wide range of signs from highway route markers to parking signs, stop signs, pedestrian crosswalk signs, and direction signs. In developing a mall, it should be determined who has charge of signage for the city or town, and who sets the design standards for these signs. Confusing signs that clutter the downtown environment should be removed as part of an overall program for central city graphics improvement.

Providing information at intersections can be simplified by combining street names and traffic signals on the same pole. This should also be more economical because fewer poles, bases, and wires are needed. Often street lighting, crosswalk directions, and trash containers can also be combined in the same unit.

These globes are mounted on 14-foot-high poles topped by Philadelphia's 1976 bicentennial symbol. (Photograph courtesy of Rohm and Haas Company.)

The lights on the Nicollet Mall, Minneapolis, are a good example of clear shades with an incandescent lamp. Each fixture has eight clear traffic lamp bulbs.

DESIGN ELEMENTS AND STREET FURNITURE

COMMERCIAL IDENTITY Signs placed on buildings to identify various shops along a mall should be considered in the overall context of the block. Each sign should be appropriate in size, scale, color, material, and message to the building's architectural character and should be placed conveniently for pedestrian viewing.

Towns and cities should develop ordinances that determine what the maximum size of signs may be, whether they may overhang onto public areas, and which type of illumination is permitted.

INFORMATIONAL SIGNS

Informational signs include directories, maps, and special signs such as those indicating the location of parking areas, subways, and bus systems. These signs give direction to the pedestrian and help him locate a particular structure such as a restaurant, department store, or office building.

SIGN MESSAGE The letter size in a message depends on the distance at which the sign is to be viewed, its location, and its lighting. Letter height should also be appropriate to the sign's setting.

LEGIBILITY The typeface should be plain in style and form, the proportion and shape familiar, and the weight heavy enough to be effective when seen from a distance.

COLOR Color is often necessary to differentiate one kind of information from another. For example, red might be used for direction, blue for information, and

San Diego pedestrian and traffic signal system.

(*Above left*) Traffic signal system used on Hamilton Mall, Allentown, Pennsylvania.

(*Left*) Directory for Gallery Place, Washington, D.C., by Arrowstreet, Inc.

green for identification. Graphics may also include banners, flags, wind socks, and other displays that add interest and color to the urban scene.

SCULPTURE

Sculpture and other works of art such as fountains and wall reliefs are important elements in improving the quality of the urban environment. These elements enhance the sensory quality of a place and help create an atmosphere where people wish to be.

Architects should meet with a sculptor in the early stages of a project to discuss the setting for a sculpture and to consult on its scale, form, mass, and color. Outdoor sculpture must have adequate mass to stand out against its background. Mass is the feeling of weight and volume that a sculpture imparts to an observer.

Size, Scale, and Form

The size and scale of a sculpture should be appropriate to its setting, which in an urban area comprises the buildings and space of which it will become an integral part. A sculpture must be large enough to

Stainless steel sculpture, "Two Columns with Wedge," by Willi Gutmann, Embarcadero Center, San Francisco.

have an impact on its surroundings. The form of a sculpture, that is, its shape and structure, will either blend or contrast with its setting. There is an infinite variety of forms that can be created in sculpture. These forms are expressed in particular materials.

Materials and Color
Materials for outdoor sculpture should be durable and resistant to urban pollution. Stone, metal, masonry, and in some cases newer materials, such as plastics, are used. Color is related to the type of material, such as granite, bronze, or stainless steel. Metals can easily be painted, and a wide range of colors is available. Plastics also offer a wide choice of colors.

A sculpture is often viewed from several directions, and the foreground as well as the background should be considered in placing the sculpture.

Orientation is also very important in relation to how and where a sculpture is placed. Sunlight and shadow patterns vary at different times of the day and with seasonal changes. There should also be enough room around the sculpture for maximum viewing from varying sight lines and for walking around it, or perhaps for viewing while sitting.

The way in which a sculpture meets the ground or sits on a base is important in terms of both its height and the way in which it is viewed. A sculpture may begin at grade or may be elevated on a base, placed in

Weathering steel sculpture by Louise Nevelson, Government Center, Binghamton, New York.

Bronze sculpture by Barbara Hepworth, Balboa Park, San Diego.

This granite sculpture also forms an area that may be walked through or used for seating.

Polished bronze and stainless steel sculpture by Arnaldo Pomodoro, Government Center, Binghamton, New York.

a planter, designed as part of a fountain, or anchored to or from a building.

Weight and installation are other important considerations in placing a sculpture. A special foundation may be needed, or equipment such as a crane may be required to set the sculpture in place.

Night Lighting

Night lighting effects on the sculpture give added interest. The location and angle of the lights, the amount of light, and the type of fixture are all important. Light may be directed from above or below, from the background or foreground, or from a combination of these.

FOUNTAINS

Fountains and pools are often the focal elements of a mall or plaza. Water, a natural element, has many unique qualities when used in fountains. The sound of water, its cooling effect, and its reflective qualities provide the designer with a wide range of creative possibilities.

Sculptural Elements

Fountains often have sculptural elements as part of their design. The sculpture acts as the focus during all

Bronze sculpture in Balboa Park, San Diego.

Polished bronze sculpture on stone base by Arnaldo Pomodoro, Hirshorn National Sculpture Garden, Washington, D.C.

Bronze sculpture on raised base in Portland, Oregon.

seasons of the year, particularly in climatic areas where water cannot be used during the winter. The orientation of the fountain determines how the reflection of sunlight off the water or on the sculptural elements will add interest.

Water Effects

The effects of water must be carefully worked out. Many different uses of sprays, jets, waterfalls, and reflecting pools are possible.

Nozzles are available in a variety of sizes and effects. By means of swivels a nozzle may be rotated about 15 degrees in all directions. This affords flexibility in aiming the water in a particular direction. An individual nozzle can use as little as 1 to 2 gallons of water per minute, depending on the desired effect. Many small fountains with the combined effects of the nozzles use several hundred gallons of water per minute, with larger ones recirculating thousands of gallons

per minute. The Civic Center Forecourt Fountain in Portland uses over 13,000 gallons per minute in its waterfall effect (see p. 161).

Fountain Details

Many factors are involved in the design of fountains.

BOTTOMS The bottoms of fountains are often painted black to add reflective qualities to the surface of a pool and to give the impression of depth. Pool bottoms may be paved with stone, brick, or tile.

Weathering steel sculpture is part of a fountain in East Liberty, Pittsburgh.

(*Above right*) **Sculpture in fountain at Ghirardelli Square, San Francisco.**

Weathering steel sculpture with use of sprays at Northeastern Bank Plaza, Scranton, Pennsylvania. (Photograph courtesy of Bellante, Clauss, Miller, and Nolan.)

EDGES, COPINGS, OR STEPS

These elements depend on the function of the fountain. Some fountains are designed for people to wade in or walk through, while other fountains are for viewing only. *COPINGS* are generally used to act as safety barriers, to define the edge of a fountain, to provide a place for sitting, and to overhang fountain equipment and thus limit the view of nozzles and water overflow controls.

MATERIALS The choice of appropriate materials for fountains is an integral part of their design. These materials must be weather and crack resistant. Poured-in-place concrete is often used to form a pool and coping. Stone, brick, or tile can be placed over concrete as a base. The materials should also be stain resistant. If weathering steel is used for a sculpture, the material and color of the fountain bottom should be chosen so as to limit problems from the stains.

Precast concrete is often used for fountain elements such as bowls from which water pours. This material is durable and crack resistant. It can also be used for copings or for pool bottoms on top of a concrete base.

Waterproofing membranes should be used to prevent water from causing problems beneath a fountain in areas with frost or on rooftops of buildings where leaks can be a critical problem. Membranes can be sprayed on or applied from rolls, as

Aerated jets in fountain at Gallery Place, Washington, D.C., by Arrowstreet, Inc.

Waterfall effect at Lovejoy Fountain, Portland, Oregon, by Lawrence Halprin and Associates.

Reflecting pool at Christian Science Church, Boston.

is roofing material, and installed in a similar manner.

MECHANICAL SYSTEMS

Mechanical systems for fountains should be designed by mechanical engineers experienced in fountain design. Mechanical systems are usually designed to allow for more capacity in gallons per minute than the minimum necessary for fountain operation so that, if a larger volume of water is desired than was originally estimated, it will be available. Pipe size should therefore be one size larger than the minimum, as should the pump, which can then be throttled down so that it does not have to run at maximum efficiency to give the desired effects. If a storage tank for recirculating water is part of the fountain equipment, it should also have reserve capacity.

PIPING Piping for fountains is generally copper with brass nozzles. If galvanized pipe is used and is connected to copper, electrolysis will result in chemical decomposition where the materials are joined. Dielectric fittings are made to limit this problem.

Drains are placed in the pool bottom for cleaning or for draining the pool to winterize it.

There are also filtering systems, chlorine injectors if people are to wade in the pools, wind controls, and automatic controls to compensate for water evaporation or spillage. A completely automatic system can be used to turn the fountain on and off at specified

Fountain bottom, paved with brick.

Fountain, Copley Square, Boston, by Sasaki Associates.

times and to control the equipment in the fountain.

A room close to or beneath the fountain will be necessary for the mechanical equipment. There must be adequate space to service this equipment easily.

Night Lighting

Night lighting gives an added effect to fountains. Lighting can be very dramatic, and sequences of different water and lighting effects can be programmed. When lights are flush with the bottom of pools, they must be winterized in cold climates. Special attention must be given to this, or the light housings may crack over the winter. Protective covers are made for some types of lights to keep them dry when the fountain is drained. The lights must also be drained and, if not covered, must be sealed with a special gasket. Lights set flush in the bottom of pools are water cooled and need at least a 2- to 3-inch depth of water above them. Lights set above pool bottoms usually require a 14-inch depth to allow for the light and for a cooling effect.

Precast bowl on fountain, Penn Square, Reading, Pennsylvania, by the Delta Group.

Night lighting on fountain, North-eastern Bank Plaza, Scranton, Pennsylvania. (Photograph courtesy of Bellante, Clauss, Miller, and Nolan.)

BOLLARDS

Bollards should be considered as an integral design element when used on a mall or plaza. They act as a barrier separating traffic from pedestrian areas. They also increase interest by setting up rhythm and providing scale, texture, and color. Bollards are often combined with chains to reinforce the feeling of separation or to help form a barrier. The use of chains also allows bollards to be spaced at a wider interval when this is necessary. Bollards often are combined with night lighting to illuminate pedestrian areas or the roadway of a semimall or transit mall.

SEATING

The type and the placement of sitting areas are important to how a mall functions. Generally, sitting areas are set back from the major circulation lines on a mall. Sitting areas should also have protection from the sun, as people prefer to sit in shaded areas.

Benches
Benches are made of wood, metal, concrete, or stone. They are usually

Bollards provide scale, texture, and color, Copley Square, Boston.

(*Above right*)
Bollard with built-in light, Penn Square, Reading, Pennsylvania.

Bollard and chains, Nicollet Mall, Minneapolis.

15 or 16 inches above grade for seating comfort and often are designed with backs. Wooden benches are the most comfortable but must be built of durable materials to limit vandalism. Concrete or stone benches, especially ones without backs, may be used in some areas of a mall and may act as sculptural elements. Benches are often combined with raised planters or walls, and in full malls are sometimes placed toward the center of the pedestrian street and separated from major circulation by the planters or walls.

In hot climates or areas directly exposed to the sun, benches are designed as parts of structures containing lattice work to provide shade.

The tops of walls or planters may also serve as sitting areas if designed at an appropriate height. This procedure can greatly expand the amount of seating on a mall.

Sitting areas, Nicollet Mall, Minneapolis.

Benches made of redwood, Northeastern Bank Plaza, Scranton, Pennsylvania. (Photograph courtesy of Bellante, Clauss, Miller, and Nolan.)

Wood bench with
back, Constitution
Plaza, Hartford,
Connecticut, by
Sasaki Associates.

Concrete and wood
bench, Penn
Square, Reading, by
the Delta Group.

Benches as sculp-
ture at Northeastern
National Life
Insurance Building,
Minneapolis.

Raised planter with built-in bench, Northeastern Bank Plaza, Scranton, Pennsylvania. (Photograph courtesy of Bellante, Clauss, Miller, and Nolan.)

Benches built into raised planter, Ithaca Commons, by Anton J. Egner and Associates.

Bench as part of trellis, Fulton Mall, by Gruen Associates.

TREE PLANTERS AND POTS

Many types of planters are available for both trees and flowers. Pots for trees must have at least a 3-foot depth and be well drained. These pots can be designed in a variety of materials such as wood, concrete and stone, or asbestos concrete. Flower pots can be placed in a variety of locations to add interest and color to urban areas. Pots are also versatile and may be moved and rearranged for special or seasonal displays.

TELEPHONES

Public telephones have been placed in a variety of enclosures or booths. Many new units are designed without booths; these provide ease of maintenance and less opportunity for vandalism. Partial weather and sound control has been studied for these newer models, and coin collection is practically vandalproof in many units.

(*Above, top*)
Flower pots, Main Street Mall, Charlottesville, Virginia.

Raised concrete planters with granite coping, Nicollet Mall, Minneapolis, by Lawrence Halprin and Associates.

Raised planters, Captain's Walk, New London, Connecticut.

KIOSKS, SHELTERS, AND CANOPIES

Kiosks, shelters, and canopies are often needed in central city areas.

Kiosks

Kiosks are well suited for pedestrian malls and have been used for bulletin boards, street directories, display cases, and information booths. They act as focal elements and also add color, help set or maintain a particular mood, and often provide night lighting.

Shelters

Shelters may be used on malls to provide sitting areas protected from the climatic factors of sunlight, wind, and precipitation. These shelters become architectural features of the mall.

BUS SHELTERS Bus shelters to provide weather protection for transit users may also be required, depending on the prevailing length of waiting time and the amount of protection from the elements offered on the street.

Some of these shelters incorporate newsstands and telephone booths and may be heated in areas with severe climates.

Canopies

Canopies have been used in the design of several malls. They provide weather protection and often act as a unifying architectural element. Appropriate choice of

Telephone booths, Hamilton Mall, Allentown, Pennsylvania.

Kiosk, Nicollet Mall, Minneapolis.

Telephone booths on the Chestnut Street Transitway, Philadelphia, are transparent and partially enclosed for privacy. (Photograph courtesy of Rohm and Haas Company.)

Kiosk, Main Street Mall, Charlottes-ville, Virginia.

Kiosk, Essex Mall, Salem, Massa-chusetts.

Shelter, Ithaca Commons. (Photograph courtesy of Anton J. Egner and Associates.)

Heated bus shelters are used on Nicollet Mall, Minneapolis.

Transparent roofed
bus shelters have
been installed on
the Chestnut Street
Transitway, Phila-
delphia.
(Photograph
courtesy of Rohm
and Haas Com-
pany.)

Canopy at Hamilton
Mall, Allentown,
Pennsylvania, by
Cope, Linder, and
Walmsley.

Canopy in downtown Wilkes-Barre, Pennsylvania, by Bohlin and Powell.

Canopy, Market Square Mall, Knoxville, Tennessee. (Photograph courtesy of Downtown Knoxville Association, Inc.)

materials, structural system, and form can help to create a certain mood or sense of place for the mall. Lighting can be incorporated into the design of the canopies and can give additional continuity to the design.

Canopies have been built with a variety of structural systems. Some have been made of steel or aluminum, some of wood, and others of concrete.

For weather protection the top of the canopy is often made of aluminum with plexiglas infill, but in some cases other materials have been used.

CLOCKS, TRASH CONTAINERS, AND DRINKING FOUNTAINS

Other items of street furniture include clocks, trash containers, and drinking fountains, all of which are part of the urban context.

Clocks

Clocks act as focal elements and add to the interest of a mall while also

Clock, Nicollet Mall, Minneapolis.

Sculptural clock tower, Fresno, California.

serving a useful function. A clock may also be a focus of a space and can act as a landmark.

Trash Containers

Trash receptacles are available in a wide variety of shapes and sizes. Many are built of wood with plastic liners; others are made of concrete, metal, or plastic.

Drinking Fountains

Drinking fountains are a functional element in pedestrian areas. They are made of many materials, such as precast concrete, metal, stone, or masonry. Fountains are also available in models that accommodate a wheelchair. Drinking fountains may also act as sculptural elements and add interest to a mall. Freezeproof types are available to limit problems in climates with frost.

Clock, Central City Mall, Williamsport, Pennsylvania.

Metal trash
container.

Concrete trash
container.

Drinking fountain
in Portland,
Oregon.

Precast concrete
drinking fountain.

Concrete drinking
fountain for the
handicapped.

5 Plants in the City

(Preceding pages)
The use of plant material is an integral part of the design concept of a mall. (Photograph courtesy of Anton J. Egner and Associates.)

In the past, many professionals in planning, architecture, and engineering considered the use of plants in urban areas mostly in terms of aesthetics. Recently, however, research has established the value of plants for climatic control, environmental engineering, and architectural uses. These uses have functional and economic benefit also.

CLIMATIC USES

Microclimate
Microclimate refers to local variations in climate, as distinguished from the climate of an overall region. Climatic factors that affect pedestrians are solar radiation, temperature, air movement, humidity, and precipitation.

SOLAR RADIATION Solar radiation provides light and heat. Much of this radiation is reflected away from the planet by clouds;

Plants control solar radiation.

part is diffused by particles in our atmosphere; some is absorbed by oxides, water vapor, and ozone; and the remainder, about 20 percent, reaches the earth's surface. Some of the solar radiation, referred to as short-wave radiation, penetrates the earth's surface and is absorbed by the ground, buildings, paving, plants, and other objects. Solar radiation heats these objects, which then reradiate heat in the form of long-wave radiation.

Control of solar radiation depends upon interception or reflection. Trees offer one of the best controls for solar radiation; they may block sunlight or filter it. Temperatures are much cooler beneath shade trees, and in effect trees provide a natural air conditioning system. This system operates with solar radiation, absorbing carbon dioxide, heat, and water and transpiring cool air in the form of water vapor. Mature trees may transpire as much as 100 gallons of water per day. This provides the cooling effect of five 10,000-British thermal unit air conditioners working 20 hours per day.

There is also a greater sense of comfort in shaded areas because of reduced long-wave radiation and lack of glare.

Scientists at the University of Indiana found that, with an air temperature of 84 degrees, the surface temperature of a concrete street was 108 degrees. Where the street was lined with trees, surface temperatures dropped 20 degrees.

WIND Wind helps to control temperatures. If wind is of low velocity, it may be pleasant. As its velocity increases, however, it may cause discomfort or damage. Plants control wind by forming barriers or obstructions, and by providing guidance, deflection, and filtration. Trees as barriers reduce windspeed by their resistance to windflow.

Urban winds are produced by convection and by constriction. Convection currents are created when air is heated by buildings, streets, and automobiles and then rises. Larger, taller buildings add greater heat to the air, causing it to rise faster and to draw air from the street toward the buildings. Convection currents usually are no problem for pedestrians.

The second effect is created by constriction of air as it travels down streets separating the linear facades of urban structures. This wind is attributed to the Venturi principle: air speeds up as a space becomes constricted. In cities the Venturi effect is determined by building height, street length, and street width.

Wind from the combined factors of convection and the Venturi effect can cause gusts felt by pedestrians. Street trees can buffer these winds at pedestrian level and filter out much of the dust and debris they stir up.

PRECIPITATION Plants help to control the amount of precipitation reaching the ground. By intercepting precipitation and slowing it down, plants aid in moisture retention and the prevention of soil erosion. They also help the soil retain its moisture by providing shade and protection from wind.

ENVIRONMENTAL ENGINEERING

Air Purification
Plants clean the air through the process of photosynthesis and the emission of oxygen. One hundred fifty square meters of leaf surface is needed to meet the yearly oxygen requirements of each person. The minimum ratio of parts of contaminated usable air for people is 1 : 3000.

Air pollution is caused by hydrocarbons, carbon oxides, sulfur oxides, photochemical oxides, thermal matter, and particulate matter.

Trees use carbon dioxide for photosynthesis. Auto exhausts account for much of the carbon dioxide in urban areas. Sulfur dioxide, also a product of fuel combustion, is prevalent in the burning of coal and in the exhausts of heating oils and automobiles. Experiments indicate that trees aid in eliminating sulfur dioxide from the air by absorption into leaves and by entrapment on their surfaces.

Ozone, a photochemical oxidant, is produced by lightning and by sunlight activating auto exhaust materials. Ozone combines readily with other substances and acts as a reagent with sulfur dioxide and ozone before they combine to form sulfuric acid. Plants aid in eliminating this dangerous pollutant.

Trees also help filter out up to 75 percent of particulate air pollutants such as dust, pollen, smoke, odors, and fumes, thus making the air more healthful for pedestrians.

Noise
Unwanted sound is referred to as noise. Noise is a problem especially in urban areas.

Sound waves are measured in cycles per second, with the range of human hearing from 20 to 20,000 cycles per second. The level of sound is measured in decibels. The sound level of a normal conversation is about 60 decibels, whereas a plane taking off may produce 120 decibels at a 200-foot distance.

Sound energy from a source usually spreads out and dissipates in transmission. Sound waves can be absorbed, reflected, deflected, or refracted. Trees absorb sound waves through their leaves, branches, and twigs. Plants with thick, fleshy leaves and thin petioles, such as the little-leaf linden, are best for this purpose. The trunks and branches of trees deflect sound, reducing the sound level. Also, wind moving through trees creates sounds that are pleasant and mask unwanted noise. It has been estimated that a 100-foot depth of forest reduces sound between the source and the observer by about 21 decibels.

Glare

Trees and shrubs reduce glare and reflection. Glare can be caused by sunlight, especially in the early morning and late afternoon, or by an artificial source such as street lights or automobile headlights. A bright light source received directly is called primary glare. Light from a primary source such as the sun causes some glare, no matter what its angle in the sky.

Reflection

Reflection of light is called secondary glare. Natural reflective surfaces are water, sand, and rock; man-made reflectors are materials such as glass, metal, chrome, brick, concrete, and painted surfaces. Atmospheric particles, which cause light to scatter, also produce secondary glare.

Plants may be used to block or filter primary glare. When the sources of glare and reflection are identified, plants having the correct size, shape, and foliage density may be placed so as to solve the problem.

Erosion Control

Plants may also be used on slopes or flat areas to prevent erosion from

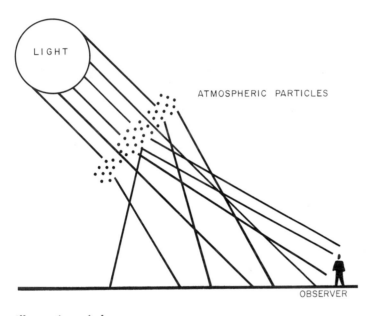

Illustration of glare.

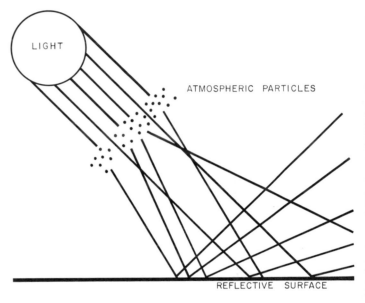

Reflection.

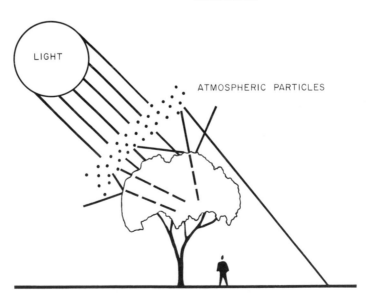

Trees block primary glare.

water runoff. Plants may be not only effective for this use but also economical as compared to the cost of paving sloped areas. Erosion is also minimized when leaves or branches intercept rain and minimize splashing, when roots hold soil, and when organic matter from plants increases soil absorption.

ARCHITECTURAL AND AESTHETIC USES

In using trees for architectural and aesthetic effects, one must consider that it takes an average of 35 years for most trees to reach maturity. The estimated average life of many buildings under construction today is 50 years. Therefore, when small trees are planted, many years pass before the trees provide an effective canopy for shade as well as other environmental and architectural benefits. For use in cities, trees with trunks 5 to 6 inches in caliper or larger are in proper scale with buildings and other elements. They also help to relate tall buildings to human scale.

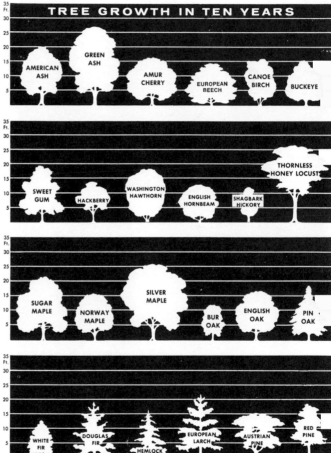

Tree growth in 10 years. (Reproduced from "How Fast Do Trees Grow?" by E. L. Kammerer, *Morton Arboretum Bulletin of Popular Information.*

Space Definition

Plants can be used as walling elements, as canopies, or as part of the base plane. As walling elements, plants can create outdoor spaces. Bosques of trees form a large canopy of shade under which sitting areas may be developed.

Screening

Trees and shrubs can screen out objectionable views. Evergreen plants are most effective for this purpose.

Continuity

Trees can provide a sense of continuity by their use in urban areas. Trees are used to line many streets in European cities, such as Paris, and to provide canopies of shaded areas in which pedestrians can walk.

Trees as Sculpture

Trees can act as sculptural elements forming the focal points of a space. Trees are interesting for their form, branch structure, texture, and color.

View Control

Trees may complement a design or provide the setting or backdrop for outdoor sculpture.

They may also provide filtered views of buildings or spaces. This filtering gives added interest and softens the urban environment of buildings and paving.

Trees also may serve to frame a view and thus maximize its dramatic effect.

In addition, plants accent architecture; for example, they reinforce

Trees form shaded outdoor spaces in Paris.

Trees provide canopies over pedestrian walks.

entry to a building or space, or they articulate space, setting up a sequence of spaces where desirable.

Mood

Plants also affect people's moods, providing privacy and a sense of springtime as new leaves unfold and flowers bloom.

CRITERIA FOR SELECTION OF PLANT MATERIAL

In selecting plant material for use in urban areas, one must be concerned with hardiness, form and structure, color, and foliage, flowers, and fruit, as well as with safety and maintenance.

Hardiness

A specific tree, shrub, or ground cover must be hardy in the region of the country where it is to be planted. Hardiness depends primarily on temperature, but precipitation and soil properties, such as degree of acidity or alkalinity, called pH, are also important items to consider. For example, sweet gums do not like temperatures below zero, and hemlocks prefer an acidic soil (see p. 76).

In what type of soil condition will the tree, shrub, or ground cover grow? For example, red maples will

Filtered view of Paley Plaza, New York, with waterfall in background, by Zion and Breen Associates, Inc.

Sculpture with backdrop of trees in Museum of Modern Art, New York.

Trees help articulate space at Central City Mall, Williamsport, Pennsylvania, by Miceli, Weed, Kulic, Inc.

grow in wet soil but also adapt to other soils; horse chestnuts need moisture, and their leaves will turn brown if the soil is too dry; dogwoods need well drained soil and cannot tolerate wet areas. Will the trees survive in city conditions? Lindens are very tolerant of air pollution, as are honey locusts and London plane trees. (See Table 5-1, pages 80 and 81.)

Does a tree provide heavy, moderate, or light shade? Does it prefer a certain exposure, such as north? Norway maples provide heavy shade, while honey locusts give light to moderate shade and filtered views. Trees in a southern exposure may thaw in winter, causing damage to some of them. Crabapples prefer a sunny exposure, as do Austrian pines, while red maples and the Douglas fir will withstand partial shade.

Is the tree free from or easily susceptible to disease or insect damage? For instance, whereas the ginkgo is virtually free of pests, birches must be sprayed for leaf miner.

Form and Structure

What are the height and the spread of the tree or shrub at maturity? What is the form of the tree—round, pyramidal, oval, upright, V-shaped, wide spreading, or weeping? Is it fast or slow in growth? Red oaks grow rapidly to about 18 feet in 10 years. Some of the most rapid growers are the plane tree, 35 feet in 10 years; the green ash, over 25

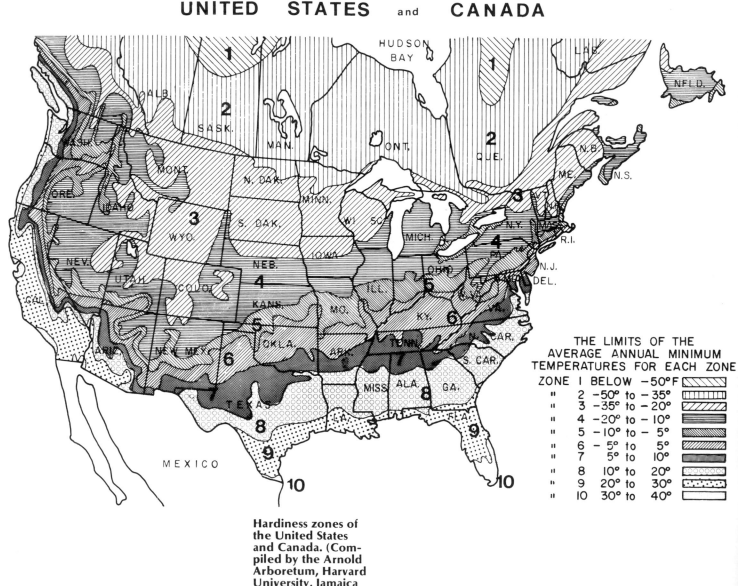

HARDINESS ZONES
of the
UNITED STATES and **CANADA**

THE LIMITS OF THE
AVERAGE ANNUAL MINIMUM
TEMPERATURES FOR EACH ZONE

ZONE	1	BELOW	$-50°F$
"	2	$-50°$ to	$-35°$
"	3	$-35°$ to	$-20°$
"	4	$-20°$ to	$-10°$
"	5	$-10°$ to	$-5°$
"	6	$-5°$ to	$5°$
"	7	$5°$ to	$10°$
"	8	$10°$ to	$20°$
"	9	$20°$ to	$30°$
"	10	$30°$ to	$40°$

Hardiness zones of the United States and Canada. (Compiled by the Arnold Arboretum, Harvard University, Jamaica Plain, Massachusetts, May 1, 1967.)

feet in 10 years; and the honey locust, over 25 feet in 10 years.

Is the plant deciduous or evergreen? Deciduous trees provide shade in summer and allow sunlight through in winter. Evergreen trees, such as Carolina hemlock or Austrian pine, make good screens. Does the tree have good branch structure and bark color? A tree such as the Amur cork tree has interesting bark and branch structure for winter effect. The London plane tree has peeling bark, which adds much interest, as do stewartias.

Foliage, Flowers, and Fruit

What are the foliage size, texture, and color? The size and texture of foliage are important design qualities. Thick, heavy foliage is good for noise reduction. Some trees have red foliage, such as the Crimson King maple or the blood-leaf Japanese maple. These trees provide added interest because of their red leaves.

Is there good autumn color? Trees with fall color are very desirable. Some examples of these are the red maple, sugar maple, red oak, pin oak, scarlet oak, dogwood, black gum, and sweet gum.

Are the flowers or fruits significant? When do they occur? Many crabapples have beautiful flowers, as well as decorative fruit. Dogwoods are also often used for their flowers, as are smaller shrubs such as azaleas.

Transplanting

Is the plant easy or difficult to transplant? Some trees, such as the scarlet oak or sweet gum, are difficult to transplant in larger sizes; others, such as the pin oak, are easily transplanted. Time of the year is also important in transplanting. For example, birches are best planted in the spring, as are magnolias.

Maintenance and Safety

Does the plant require spraying for insects or removing litter from seed pods or leaves? Trees such as birches and crabapples need to be sprayed for insect control. Other trees, such as the horse chestnut, catalpa, and native honey locust, drop seed pods or fruit. The female ginkgo has particularly obnoxious smelling fruit, and the male variety should be chosen.

Is the plant weak wooded, is it easily susceptible to insects or disease, or does it have thorns? Trees that tend to split in windy conditions are undesirable along streets, and there may be an ordinance against their use in some cities. An example is the silver maple, which is weak wooded and prone to damage in storms. A few trees, such as hawthorns and native honey locusts, have thorns, which may cause problems. Thornless and seedless varieties of honey locust that are also resistant to disease are available.

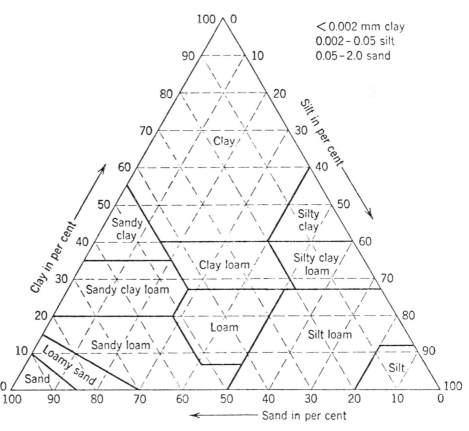

Soil classification chart: U.S. Agriculture Department.

Some evergreen trees will grow in some cities, but where industrial pollution is high they may not survive because of particulates that remain on the leaves for more than 1 year, interfering with growth.

PLANTING PROCEDURES

Soil Composition

Soil is composed of mineral and organic matter, water, and air. Three mineral particles and one organic particle affect soil texture. Sand is the largest (0.05 to 2.0 millimeters) mineral particle. Sand increases aeration and drainage but has little moisture holding capacity. Silt, a smaller (0.002 to 0.05 millimeter) particle increases moisture holding capacity, and clay, the smallest soil particle (0.002 millimeter and smaller), increases nutrient holding capacity. Organic matter averages 3 to 5 percent in topsoil, and it keeps soil loose and porous. A sandy loam will be about 60 percent sand, 25 percent silt, and 15 percent clay.

Soil Tests

Topsoil must be tested at a laboratory for pH. Where necessary, the acidity or alkalinity range of the soil required by a plant must be adjusted. The pH scale extends from 0 to 14, with a pH value of 7 being neutral, below 7 acidic, and above 7 alkaline. The pH scale is logarithmic, and changing from pH 7 to pH 8 means 10 times more alkaline, while

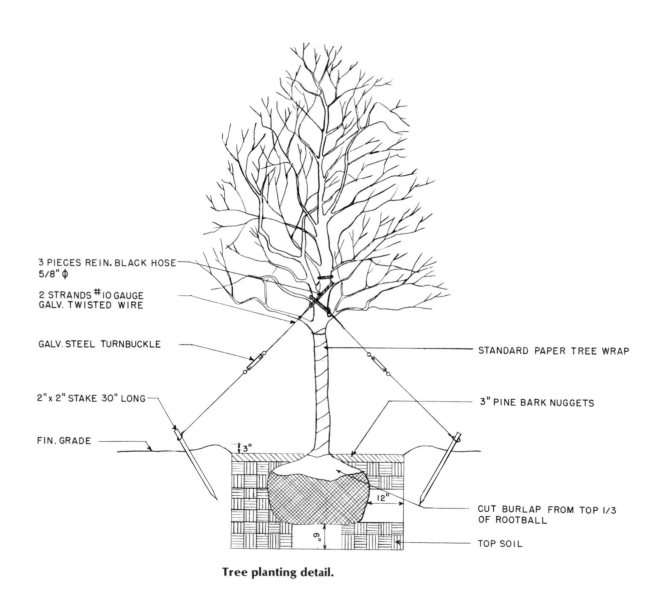

3 PIECES REIN. BLACK HOSE 5/8" ⌀

2 STRANDS #10 GAUGE GALV. TWISTED WIRE

GALV. STEEL TURNBUCKLE

2" x 2" STAKE 30" LONG

FIN. GRADE

3"

12"

9"

STANDARD PAPER TREE WRAP

3" PINE BARK NUGGETS

CUT BURLAP FROM TOP 1/3 OF ROOTBALL

TOP SOIL

Tree planting detail.

going from pH 6.5 to pH 4.5 means that the soil is 100 times more acidic. Most plants need a pH of 6 to 6.5. Some plants, such as the red oak, however, will grow in a more acidic soil with a pH of 5.5 or less.

Soil pH is also important because it is related to nutrient availability. Plants absorb nutrients from the soil in liquid form. Nutrients are most readily available in soil with a nearly neutral pH.

Soil can also be tested for organic content and required nutrients—nitrogen, potassium, phosphorus, and trace elements such as manganese and iron.

Tree Pits

Tree pits should be excavated to a 5-foot diameter and to a minimum depth of 4 feet and should be backfilled with a topsoil mix. The topsoil should drain well after watering. A typical mix would be one third screened topsoil, one third coarse sand, and one third peat moss.

Planting and Guying

A tree is generally dug at the nursery with an earth ball, which is burlapped and tied with rope to keep it from breaking. When the tree is planted, the topsoil should be no higher than the tree was when growing at the nursery. This would be a few inches above the burlapped ball. After the tree is planted, it should be well watered to remove air pockets in the soil.

A tree is guyed to prevent movement of the tree from breaking the earth ball and shifting the root system out of the original ball. Such movement can be detrimental to tree growth. Galvanized steel guy wires are placed through rubber hose and fastened around the tree. They are then tied to stakes or deadmen placed in the ground, eyelets fastened to sidewalk blocks, or cedar stakes placed vertically adjacent to the tree. Turnbuckles are often used to tighten guy wires.

Wrapping

After the tree is planted, the trunk should be wrapped with tree paper or good quality burlap up to the first major branch. The purpose of the tree wrap is to prevent sun scald of some species, such as sugar maple, and to reduce evaporation through the trunk. The trunk should be inspected for wounds or insect damage before the tree is wrapped.

Pruning

Pruning the newly planted tree helps keep the evaporation of water in balance with the retention capacity of the roots, which have been cut back to the root ball. Depending upon the form and structure of the tree, about one third of the branches should be cut back.

Mulch

Generally, after the tree is guyed and watered, a mulch of peat moss or wood chips about 3 inches deep is applied from the trunk of the tree to the edge of the excavation to help the root system retain moisture.

Saucer

A saucer about 3 inches high is then created around the tree to retain moisture after watering.

Planting Dates

Planting dates vary with the local seasons and the type of tree. Some trees do better when planted in the spring. These trees, if deciduous, should be planted before the new leaves come out. If trees are balled before the leaves come out, they may be stored until ready for planting. After leaves develop, special precautions must be taken when moving the trees, and there is a high chance that losses will occur. Deciduous trees can also be moved in the fall after the first hard frost.

Evergreen trees can be planted in the spring or late summer. They should be moved in the spring before new growth progresses, or at the end of the summer when new growth has hardened, temperatures have cooled, and the soil is of proper consistency for digging the earth balls. This is usually the end of August to the middle of September. Evergreens generally prefer acidic soil, and organic materials such as peat moss are added to the topsoil.

Maintenance

When trees are planted in the city, they need care in the form of pruning, watering, fertilizing, and spraying to prevent fungus or insect damage. Tree grates (see p. 41) also help in allowing rain water to reach the tree while preventing compaction of soil by pedestrians. The tree grate should be at least 4 feet square in size.

Problems from snow removal must also be considered. If chemicals are used, sodium nitrate is preferred instead of sodium or calcium chloride.

Trees can be raised above sidewalk areas by means of curbs or raised tree planters. If raised tree planters are used, winter injury to the roots of plants in the containers may be a problem. Roots are more sensitive to low temperatures than are upper portions of a plant. Insulation on the walls of the planter may help prevent injury to the roots.

Raised planters must also have good drainage and, when used on rooftop areas, must contain drains. The drain usually has about 3 inches of gravel above it and is separated from the topsoil mix by a fiberglass mat.

TABLE 5-1

Trees for City Use

Latin Name	Common Name	Hardiness Zone	Height (feet)	Habit*	Fall Colors	Characteristics
		DECIDUOUS TREES				
Acer platanoides var.	Norway Maple	3	60	O	Yellow	Dense foliage
Acer platanoides Crimson King	Crimson King	3	60	O		Purple foliage
Acer platanoides Emerald Queen	Emerald Queen	3	60	O	Yellow	Rapid growth
Acer platanoides summershade	Summershade	3	65	O		Dark green foliage
Acer platanoides pseudoplatanus	Sycamore Maple	5	80	WS		Winged fruit
Carpinus betulus	European Hornbeam	5	30	P	Yellow	Dense foliage
Crataegus phaenopyrum	Washington Hawthorn	4	25	R	Scarlet-orange	White flowers and orange berries
Fraxinus pennsylvanica lanceolata var.	Green Ash	2	60	R	Yellow	Rapid growth
Fraxinus p. lanceolata Marshall's Seedless Ash	Marshall's Seedless Ash	2	55	R	Yellow	Dark green foliage
Ginkgo biloba var.	Ginkgo	4	75	R	Yellow	Disease resistant
Ginkgo biloba Autumn Gold	Autumn Gold	4	45	U	Yellow	Male
Ginkgo biloba Fairmount	Fairmount	4	75	P	Yellow	Male
Ginkgo biloba Lakeview	Lakeview	4	50	U	Yellow	Male
Ginkgo biloba Princeton Sentry	Princeton Sentry	4	70	U	Yellow	Male
Gleditsia triancanthos inermis var.	Thornless Honey Locust	4	70	WS	Yellow	
Gleditsia t. inermis Imperial	Imperial	4	35	WS	Yellow	Dense foliage
Gleditsia t. inermis Majestic	Majestic	4	65	V	Yellow	Dark green foliage
Gleditsia t. inermis Moraine	Moraine	4	80	V	Yellow	
Gleditsia t. inermis Shademaster	Shademaster	4	40	R	Yellow	Disease resistant
Gleditsia t. inermis Skyline	Skyline	4	45	P	Yellow	Leathery foliage
Gleditsia t. inermis Sunburst	Sunburst	4	35	WS	Yellow	Yellow foliage on branch tip
Koelreuteria paniculata	Goldenrain Tree	4	30	R		Yellow flower
Liquidambar styraciflua var.	Sweet Gum	5	60	P	Scarlet	Disease resistant
Liquidambar styraciflua Burgundy	Burgundy	5	60	P	Purple	
Liquidambar styraciflua Festival	Festival	5	60	U	Red-yellow	
Liquidambar styraciflua Moraine	Moraine	5	60	O	Scarlet	Fast growth
Magnolia soulangeana	Saucer Magnolia	5	20	R	Bronze	Shrublike, white flowers
Magnolia stellata	Star Magnolia	5	20	R	Orange	Shrublike, white flowers
Malus var.	Crabapple					
Malus American Beauty	American Beauty	4	20	U		Red flowers Red fruit
Malus baccata	Siberian Crab	2	25	U		White flowers Red-yellow fruit
Malus floribunda	Japanese Flowering Crab	4	25	P	Yellow-orange	Pink-white flowers Red-yellow fruit
Malus hupensis	Tea Crab	4	20	V		Pink flowers Yellow-red fruit
Malus sargenti	Sargent Crab	5	8	R		White flowers Dark red fruit
Malus Snowdrift	Snowdrift Crab	3	20	R		White flowers Orange-red fruit
Malus zumi calocarpa	Zumi Crab	4	15	P		White flowers Red fruit

* O: oval, P: pyramidal, R: round, U: upright, W: weeping, V: vase-shaped, WS: wide-spreading.

TABLE 5-1 (*Continued*)

Latin Name	Common Name	Hardiness Zone	Height (feet)	Habit*	Fall Colors	Characteristics
		DECIDUOUS TREES (*Continued*)				
Phellodendron amurense	Amur Cork Tree	3	45	WS	Yellow	Interesting corky bark
Platanus acerifolia var.	London Plane Tree	5	80	WS		Peeling bark
Platanus acerifolia Bloodgood	Bloodgood	5	50	WS		Disease resistant
Pyrus calleryana var.	Callery Pear	5	30	P	Red	White flowers
Pyrus calleryana Aristocrat	Aristocrat	5	40	O	Crimson	Large foliage
Pyrus calleryana Bradford	Bradford	5	40	P	Crimson	Thornless
Pyrus calleryana Chanticleer	Chanticleer	5	40	P	Yellow	Rapid growth
Pyrus calleryana Fauriei	Fauriei	5	15	R		Dwarf selec.
Quercus borealis	Red Oak	4	75	R	Red	Rapid growth
Quercus laurifolia	Laurel Oak	7	60	R		Dense foliage
Quercus palustris var. sovereign	Sovereign Pin Oak	4	75	P	Red	Branching horizontally or ascending
Quercus phellos	Willow Oak	5	50	R	Yellow	Willowlike foliage
Sabal palmetto	Cabbage Palmetto	8	90	Palm		
Salix babylonica	Babylon Weeping Willow	5	40	W	Yellow	Pendulous
Sophora japonica	Japanese Pagoda Tree	4	70	R	Yellow	
Tilia cordata var.	Little-leaf Linden	3	60	P	Yellow	Disease resistant Leathery foliage
Tilia cordata Greenspire	Greenspire Linden	3	60	P	Yellow	Disease resistant Leathery foliage
Tilia cordata Chancellor	Chancellor Linden	3	60	P	Yellow	Dense foliage
Tilia europaea	European Linden	3	60	R	Yellow	
Ulmus americana var. Augustine	Augustine Ascending Elm	2	90	V		Susceptible to Dutch elm disease and necrosis
Ulmus carpinifolia Christine Buisman	Christine Buisman Elm	4	60	V		
Zelkova serrata var.	Japanese Zelkova	5	60	V	Yellow-Russet	
Zelkova Parkview	Parkview	5	60	V	Russet	Disease resistant, consistent form
Zelkova Village Green	Village Green	5	60	V	Russet	Disease resistant, rapid growth
		EVERGREEN TREES				
Abies concolor	White Fir	4	100	P		Blue-green foliage
Cinnamomum camphora	Camphor	9	40	R		Dense, glossy foliage
Magnolia grandiflora	Southern Magnolia	7	100	P		White flowers
Picea pungens	Colorado Spruce	2	80	P		Stiff green to blue foliage
Quercus virginiana	Live Oak	7	60	WS		Fine textured foliage
Taxus cuspidata	Japanese Yew	4	30	P		Red berries
Tsuga caroliniana	Carolina Hemlock	4	75	P		Dense, needlelike foliage

* O: oval, P: pyramidal, R: round, U: upright, W: weeping, V: vase-shaped, WS: wide-spreading.

6 Case Studies

(*Preceding pages*)
Construction of Ithaca Commons. (Photograph courtesy of Anton J. Egner and Associates.)

To examine in depth the design features and development strategies of malls, case studies of full malls, transit malls, and semimalls are presented in this chapter. These examples provide an overview of malls that have been built in the United States and Canada in the past 20 years.

During this period (as now) many central city shopping areas needed to be revitalized in order to compete with suburban shopping centers. There were problems such as traffic congestion, pollution, lack of adequate parking, and deterioration of buildings and the economic base in many downtowns.

These factors, as well as the desire to provide a pleasant environment for urban shoppers, led to the development of malls in many cities, beginning in Kalamazoo, Michigan, in 1959. Many of these malls have features such as fountains, sculpture, new paving, planting, sitting areas, children's play areas, night lighting, and comfort stations, and

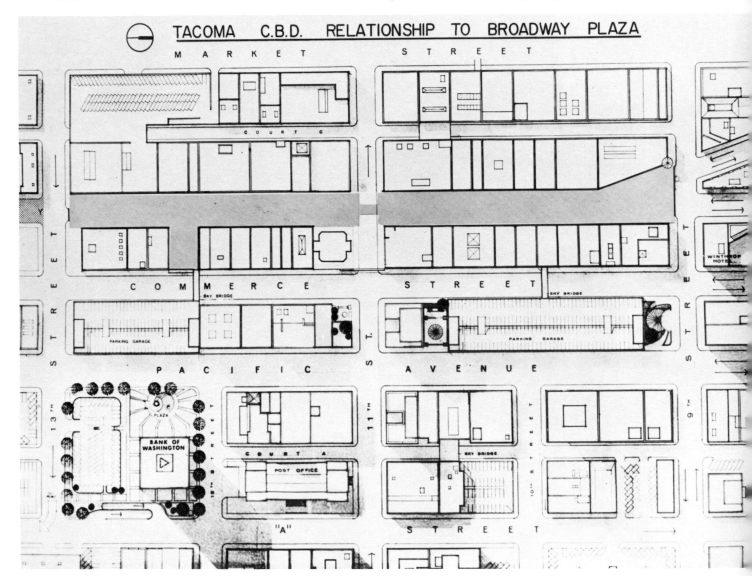

Relationship of central business district to mall. (Photographs courtesy of Tacoma Community Development Department.)

are centers for promotional and cultural events.

These malls have been financed in a variety of ways by Federal Urban Renewal Agency funds; by assessment districts; by the city, county, and state; by the Urban Mass Transportation Administration; by Community Development Program Funds; by private donations; and by other programs as funds become available.

Providing a pleasant environment for retail sales (including good access and parking) increases investor confidence, which spurs new construction in the downtown and broadens the tax base. Many of the malls have been successful at reversing the decline of retail sales in the downtowns and have encouraged pedestrian use by providing separation of vehicular and pedestrian circulation, or by expanding walks substantially and creating an urban environment with amenities and activities that attract people.

Broadway Plaza

TACOMA, WASHINGTON

Architects

HARRIS AND REED, AND LITZENBERGER AND JAMES McGRANAHAN

Description

Broadway Plaza is a full mall located in downtown Tacoma, Washington, a city with a population of 157,000 people, 25 miles south of Seattle. The mall was developed to revital-

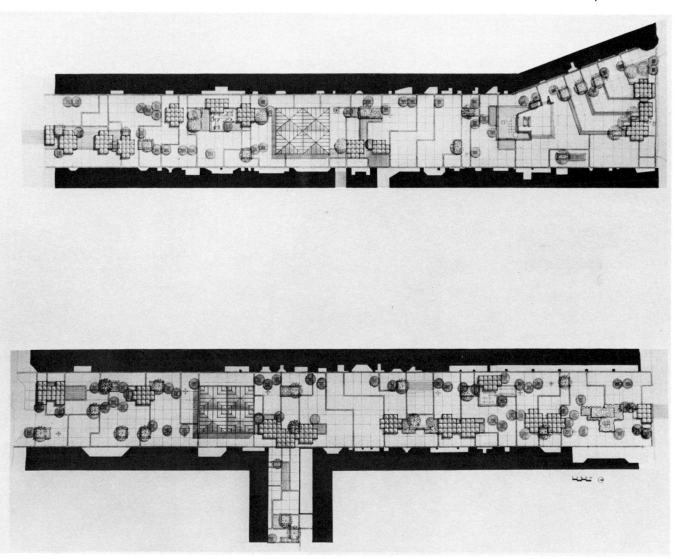

Plan of mall.

ize the downtown and create a pedestrian precinct. Broadway Plaza extends for two double blocks (1380 feet) and is 80 feet wide.

Design features include large covered areas that serve as bus stops and rest areas, as well as fountains, pools, performing and display stages, two children's play areas, lighting, and planting. About one fourth of the mall is under cover, and there is seating capacity for 1500 people.

The first phase of the mall was financed by Federal Urban Renewal Agency funds, including noncash city matching funds. The mall was completed in May, 1974, at a cost of $1.5 million, the extension being funded by an Economic Development Administration grant.

Development Strategy

The plaza was proposed in 1944, but serious planning did not begin until the mid-1960s.

A team management approach was utilized in the planning, design, and implementation of the Broadway Plaza. A unique partnership between the private and public sectors evolved, from which came not only the plaza but also two parking structures built with little cost to the city. A gift of $4 million worth of garages to the city by the private sector generated over $13 million in federal grants.

A team of representatives from all city departments, private utilities, private businesses, and public officials was established. The team's first objective was to select a design concept and define program requirements. An architectural team of two firms on a joint venture basis was selected.

Public hearings were held which gave citizens a chance to review plans and offer opinions. A storefront office was also manned for two Saturdays to talk with people about the design and to listen to suggestions. On two occa-

sions the city closed the street to all traffic to test the impact on the surrounding area.

Program development also required conformance with a detailed state law on pedestrian malls. Numerous legal requirements had to be met and resolved, as Broadway Plaza was the first pedestrian mall to be built in the state.

Design Features

CANOPIES The mall has large covered areas under which people may walk, sit, or wait for buses. These structures have clear plexi-glass elements to allow a light, open feeling.

FOUNTAINS The plaza features several fountains with aerated jets of water and pools formed by concrete walls.

PAVING The base plane of the plaza is paved predominantly in concrete with brick bands. A few

Photograph of street before the mall was developed, looking from 9th Street south.

CENTRAL CITY MALLS

larger areas of brick paving are also used.

LIGHTING Night lighting is provided by clusters of clear, round acrylic globes on metal standards.

SITTING AREAS Seating is available for approximately 1500 people. Benches are provided, along with built-in seating around fountains and in two children's play areas.

PLANTING Landscaping consists of about 75 trees and over 4000 other plants.

In Retrospect

The plaza is becoming the site of a festival of events, such as auto and boat shows, bake sales, art shows, and music festivals. The team approach so effective in developing the plaza has been used to get other projects started.

Sales have increased, and a double-block extension of the mall, which will be a semimall, is to be completed in 1977.

View of mall logo and canopy.

Completed fountain.

(*Opposite page*)
**Overall view of mall
canopy system and
paving.**

Captain's Walk

NEW LONDON, CONNECTICUT

Landscape Architects
JOHNSON AND DEE

Description

Captain's Walk is located on State Street in New London, Connecticut, the core city within the southeastern Connecticut region. Although New London has a population of only 31,360, it serves a region of 225,000 people.

A semimall was chosen to meet the need for a physical plan that could be produced at a cost in scale with the downtown economy.

The semimall is six blocks in length, with one-way traffic on the lower portion between O'Neill Drive and Water Street. The upper blocks have two-way traffic between Huntington and Washington Streets. However, traffic is prohibited from the central portion of the mall, which is oriented toward pedestrians and has only emergency and service vehicle access on a 12-foot-wide curvilinear path.

The mall features a nautical theme that reflects the past history of New London as a seaport, whaling town, and sailors' port-of-call. Street lights, bollards, and canopy structures are painted white. New paving, grass islands, trees, shrubs, and sitting areas have also been provided.

Captain's Walk was developed with funds from the Downtown New London Association, the Federal

View of mall, showing paving, canopies, and other features.

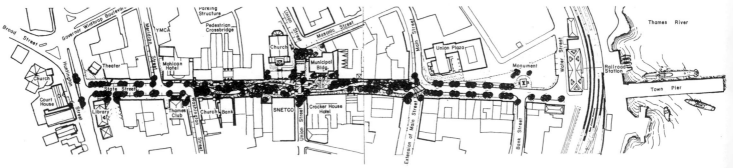

Plan of mall.

Urban Renewal Agency, and the state. The project was completed in November, 1973, at a cost of $1.5 million.

Development Strategy

A pedestrian mall concept was exhibited in early 1969. This design included pedestrian and vehicular circulation systems, parking locations, service access, staging, and environmental improvements. The proposal became part of the Winthrop Urban Renewal Project.

A full mall concept was abandoned in 1971 because of uncertainties about federal funding and inability to resolve legal and service problems.

The semimall was then selected as the scheme most appropriate to the physical setting. The objective of the design was to create a new setting that would provide visual excitement and a new identity for the downtown. Also, State Street had high quality shops and professional, banking, and financial services for

the region, which the mall would complement and strengthen. The Downtown New London Association raised $50,000 in voluntary funds, based on a benefit assessment formula, as seed money to get the project started. Once this commitment had been obtained, the City Council endorsed the project and formal applications were made. Funding was provided by the Federal Urban Renewal Agency and by the state.

In addition to the semimall, in

Canopies appear as abstract sails and have night lighting with clear round globes.

November, 1970 the Governor Winthrop parking garage was opened. It provides 406 parking spaces and features a covered pedestrian bridge that links directly to Captain's Walk. Another 205 municipal parking spaces were upgraded in 1973, and ground-breaking took place for a 550-car garage in the lower Captain's Walk area.

Design Features

PAVING Bomanite, a deep brown concrete, was used and stamped with a metal form to create a cobblestone-like appearance. This material extends the full width of the mall. Some people like the paving texture, but others object to its roughness.

CANOPIES Canopies are made of white pipe frame and fiberglass and provide shelter for exhibits and concessions.
They are built in a modular fashion and can be expanded if desired.

PLANTING As part of the mall, a series of mounded grass islands, nicknamed "whales," are planted with trees. Other planters are round wood tubs; these are used as accents.

NIGHT LIGHTING Street lighting has been raised to a minimum of 5 footcandles to provide a safe and secure atmosphere. The street lights are 35 feet high, with clear globes and 100-watt deluxe white mercury bulbs.

Mounded grass islands have coping at sitting height.

Round wood planters.

Lights on 10-foot black poles with clear globes and 175-watt bulbs are placed in the islands with the trees. These lights are used for special events.

PLANTING Plant materials used in the mall are honey locusts, red oaks, maples, shrubs, and flowers. Grass is also used in the mounded islands.

OTHER FURNISHINGS These furnishings include bollards, a clock, code and signal flags, and graphics on the canopies.

In Retrospect

The semimall has brought new shoppers into the city, sales have increased, and the merchants and the community have developed a pride in the downtown. There has also been substantial new investment in properties along the mall. In addition, as previously described, much new parking has been added in the downtown area that serves the mall.

View of canopy lighting.

View showing canopy, lights, and clock.

Chestnut Street Transitway

PHILADELPHIA, PENNSYLVANIA

Architects and Planners
UELAND AND JUNKER

Engineers
De LEUW, CATHER

Landscape Architectural Consultant
EUGENE De SILLETS

Description

The Chestnut Street Transitway is located along one of Philadelphia's busiest downtown shopping streets in a city with a population of 1,861,719. The transitway mall is 12 blocks long, stretching from 6th to 18th Streets. Generally, the mall is 60 feet in width, but between 9th and 10th Streets it is wider because of the setback of federal buildings. Traffic on the transitway is limited to buses on a 20-foot-wide roadway. After 6:00 P.M. taxicabs are allowed.

The mall is a shopping promenade and features expanded sidewalks with new paving, pedestrian crosswalks at midblock, specially designed lighting with bicentennial theme elements attached to light standards, bus shelters, raised planters, and some seating. Efficient transit was a dominant goal of the development plans, and so application was made for federal funding. The project was funded by the Urban Mass Transportation Administration, the city, and the

state. The transitway was completed in June, 1976, at a cost of $7.4 million.

Development Strategy
In the mid-1960s, the city government had feasibility studies made on turning Chestnut Street into a pedestrian mall. The Chestnut Street Association, founded by merchants on and near the street, voiced strong objections, and the concept was not developed further. However, the following decade was marked by an increasing number of middle class residents commuting to work, a fuel crisis, and shifting urban patterns that resulted in heavier use of the public transit system. Merchants began changing their attitudes toward upgrading Chestnut Street, and city officials approached them with the concept of a transit mall.

Also, Philadelphia '76, Inc., the city's bicentennial organization, was seeking transportation alternatives to move visitors easily between the historic area, on the east side of center city, and the permanent museums along the Benjamin Franklin Parkway to the west.

Architects worked on a concept with Philadelphia '76, Inc., and were then retained by a committee of Chestnut Street merchants to develop the design of the transit mall. In March, 1974, the plan was approved by the general membership of the Chestnut Street Association, even though some opposition was voiced by parking lot owners along the street, who feared that their businesses would suffer from removal of automobile traffic.

Funding was approved by the Urban Mass Transportation Administration for 80 percent of the $7.4 million cost. The remainder was split by the city and the state.

The city and bicentennial officials promised merchants that construction of the mall would not disrupt Christmas shopping and that it would be completed by April, 1976. When the street was closed to traffic and construction began, there were few problems. Traffic studies showed that Market Street had unused capacity and could handle much of the rerouted traffic. Also, parking was banned for a block in either direction on streets intersecting with Chestnut to allow service zones for truck delivery. Some nighttime loading is allowed on the transitway by special permit.

Design Features
PAVING Walks have been increased to 20 feet in width on each side of the roadway. Sidewalk areas are paved predominantly in brick, with concrete adjacent to building facades and in the crosswalk pattern at midblock. Curbs fade out at crosswalk areas for ease of pedestrian use.

LIGHTING Night lighting was specially designed for the mall.

(*Opposite page*)
Typical view of mall. (Photograph courtesy of Rohm and Haas Company.)

View of crosswalk area at midblock, including traffic controls. (Photograph courtesy of Rohm and Haas Company.)

Clusters of eight luminous globes of smoky gray acrylic plastic are placed on 14-foot-high anodized bronze aluminum poles. Bicentennial elements were also attached to the tops of the poles.

Other illumination is provided by high level lights on 28-foot poles. These lights use 400-watt high pressure sodium lamps. There are also lights included in the pedestrian signals at midblock areas.

BUS SHELTERS Large, transparent, roofed bus shelters are provided. They are free standing and take up minimal space both physically and visually.

PLANTING Trees are planted both directly in the sidewalk areas and in raised tree planters. Grates are used around the trees placed in walk areas.

SEATING Benches in a small sitting area are provided in conjunction with the midblock crosswalk area. These benches are limited to about four per block. Trash receptacles are also placed near the benches (perhaps too close), as well as in other locations.

In Retrospect

The transitway has improved pedestrian circulation on Chestnut Street, and merchants seem to be happy with the results of the mall. Since the street is only 60 feet in width for most of its length, a few wider spaces adjacent to the mall would provide added room for feature elements and places for people to sit.

View of crosswalk and sidewalk areas. (Photograph courtesy of Ueland and Junker.)

CENTRAL CITY MALLS

A 24-inch clear Plexiglas cube is placed on each traffic control column. Each cube contains a 50-watt mercury vapor lamp. (Photograph courtesy of Rohm and Haas Company.)

Sitting areas. (Photograph courtesy of Rohm and Haas Company.)

Typical 28-foot high pressure sodium light. (Photograph courtesy of Rohm and Haas Company.)

City Center Mall

EUGENE, OREGON

Landscape Architects
MITCHELL, McARTHUR, GARDINER AND O'KANE

Architects
MORIN, LONGWOOD, AND EDLUND

Planners
GEORGE ROCKRISE AND ASSOCIATES

Description

City Center Mall is located in Eugene, Oregon, a city of 79,028 residents. It establishes a pedestrian precinct in an eight-block area, replacing the vehicular emphasis of former city streets. The initial stage included five city blocks of what was once part of Broadway and Willamette Street in downtown Eugene. The other three blocks will include Willamette to 8th Avenue, and will add two blocks on Olive. The existing streets for the mall have a right-of-way of 66 feet and feature the Central Plaza at Broadway and Willamette, with a fountain as its focus, new paving of brick and concrete, play areas with rest room facilities, planting, night lighting, sitting areas, and a partially covered walkway at midblock leading to parking facilities.

The project was accomplished with urban renewal funds from the federal government. The first phase was completed in 1971 at a cost of $1.3 million.

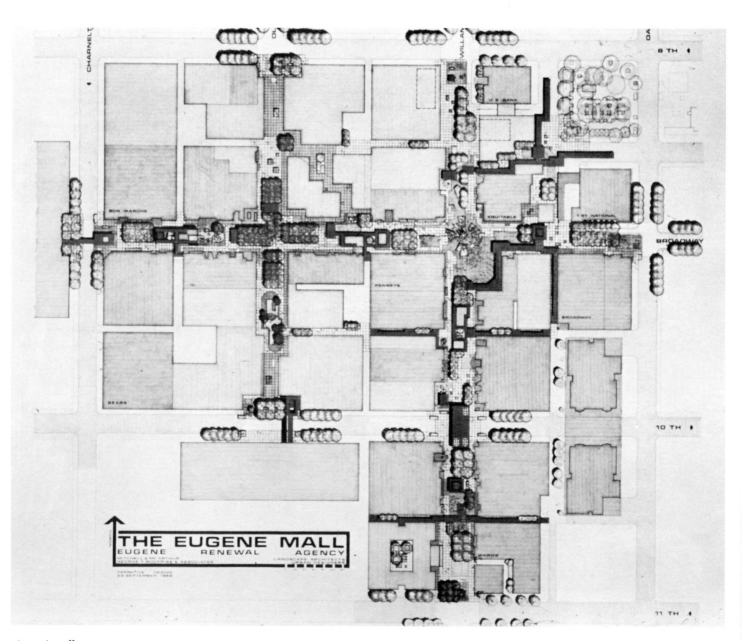

Plan of mall.
(Photographs courtesy of Mitchell Associates.)

Development Strategy

The primary objectives of the downtown renewal were to improve the area through redevelopment and rehabilitation of substandard buildings, to eliminate blight, to modify the street system, to provide adequate parking, and to create traffic-free pedestrian precincts. Also, it was believed that these improvements would stimulate private investment in new development, protect the existing economic base, and provide an increase in taxes for the city and county.

Under provisions of state legislation enacted in 1957, the mayor and the City Council started the Urban Renewal Agency of Eugene. After several trips to California to review renewal projects, civic leaders became enthusiastic about federally assisted renewal programs and began the efforts that led to the mall.

In 1965 the City Council appointed a six-member group of citizens to serve as the Eugene Development Commission. In 1967 a seventh member was added, and the commission became the Urban Renewal Agency of Eugene.

In the late 1960s the city applied for planning funds from the Department of Housing and Urban Development (HUD). Once the funds were approved, an 18-month planning effort began, involving officials, citizens, and urban planners. After public meetings the plan was adopted by the City Council in December, 1968. In March, 1969, the federal government approved the project.

Citizen-Community Involvement

The spring of 1966 was marked by Eugene's Conference on Community Goals, involving several hundred residents taking part in three meetings. From these meetings, statements evolved that were adopted by the City Council as the official community goals and policies.

A 100-member citizens' advisory committee (SCORE: Special Committee on Renewing Eugene) was established in October, 1966. The members appointed by the mayor included businessmen, educators, professionals, tradesmen, and housewives. Meetings were held in city council chambers, and citizens were invited.

During the survey and planning phase conducted by the planning consultants SCORE met more than a dozen times. Final decisions were made by the Planning Review Committee, which consisted of seven SCORE members, the mayor and the City Council, the Eugene Planning Commission, and The Eugene Urban Renewal Agency members. The Planning Review Committee held several meetings with the architectural consultants, and all meetings were open to the public. Several subcommittees of SCORE provided advice and technical assistance in regard to historic structures, urban design, and socioeconomic concerns.

Social, Economic, and Environmental Considerations

The physical form of the mall resulted from objectives developed by the community. These objectives were as follows:

1. An attractive design unique to Eugene.
2. An attractive and competitive retail market offering a diversity of goods.
3. Separation of pedestrian and vehicular traffic.
4. Elimination of nonessential vehicular traffic.
5. Adequate parking, separate from pedestrian areas.
6. Improved public transportation service to the city center.
7. Protection from the weather for pedestrians.
8. A lively atmosphere.
9. A place of contact for all groups of the metropolitan population.
10. A mix of activities that could not flourish in other locations.

Design Features

FOUNTAINS Central Plaza at Broadway and Willamette is the focal point of the mall and serves as a gathering place. It has a water feature consisting of 37 concrete elements, the highest of which is 25 feet. Water cascades over the blocks into a series of pools at a rate of 3400 gallons a minute. The fountain invites pedestrians to walk through it or sit on its concrete walls. A second-level viewing platform is at the southeast corner of the plaza. The fountain is intended to symbolize the mountains and streams of Oregon.

A landscaped plaza at Broadway and Olive has a circular water feature, which serves as the focal point for a more intimate plaza, oriented to quiet activities. It has sitting areas and also contains small game tables with built-in checker boards.

PLAY AREAS Two play areas in portions of the mall stimulate creative play and have adjacent rest rooms.

PAVING AND MATERIALS Entry areas announce the mall by means of kiosks, lawn panels, brick, bollards, and a bosque of trees. A grid paving pattern of brick and concrete is used on portions of the mall. To avoid large warped areas, there is a continuous trench drain with a brick cover.

PLANTING Plant materials were selected to provide seasonal color, soften the harsh lines of adjacent elements, provide screening, develop spaces, and minimize maintenance. Tree grates and guards are used around trees for protection and added interest.

MALL LIGHTING Lighting provides a warm but uneven level of illumination, making the mall an inviting place to be. Trees are uplighted, and entrances and focal elements are also lighted, although store windows are maintained as the main light source.

SERVICE Service to the mall is provided from courts in the center of the mall, accessible from alleys.

MAINTENANCE Complete maintenance is provided by the Eugene Parks and Recreation Department. Lawns and landscaped areas are trimmed and irrigated and fertilized.

In Retrospect
The mall inspires favorable comments from visitors, and the majority of Eugene residents find shopping more pleasant. The mall has also generated renovation of buildings, along with new development that extends pedestrian circulation through private property. In addition, the city of Eugene, since October, 1973, has provided the general public with free unlimited-time parking in the downtown. The parking district comprises an area of 15 square blocks within 2 blocks of

the mall. Employers and employees of businesses cannot use these lots. The cost of this program is paid for by property owners, businesses, and professionals.

The free customer parking and the mall have helped put the CBD on a competitive basis with outlying regional shopping centers. This has shown the public that the CBD is not going to be replaced by suburban shopping centers.

Bosque of trees with tree grates and guards integrated into the paving pattern.

(*Opposite page*)
View of fountain.

WALK

View of paving pattern, lighting, seating, and other mall features.

Fort Street Mall

HONOLULU, HAWAII

Architects
VICTOR GRUEN ASSOCIATES

Description

The Fort Street Mall is located in downtown Honolulu, Hawaii, a city of 324,871 residents. The mall is five blocks (1738 feet) in length, extending from Queen Street to Beretania Street. It averages 50 feet in width, but at the King Street Plaza it widens to 88 feet and at Father Damien Plaza Beretania Street becomes 93 feet wide. There are cross streets at Hotel and Merchant with a pedestrian underpass at King Street. The mall features include two pools, fountains, a waterfall, planters, a children's sandbox, four archways to support flowering vines, night lighting, and a special mural in the King Street underpass.

The project was funded by the city and county for 55 percent of the total, by private property owners for 44 percent, and by the Board of Water Supply for 1 percent.

Mall construction began in June, 1968, and was completed by February, 1969, at a cost of $2.7 million.

Development Strategy

In the late 1940s a few individuals foresaw the decline of downtown Honolulu and made proposals to ensure its position as the center of retail and business activity in the area.

In 1949 the Hawaii Chapter of the American Institute of Architects made the first proposal to close Fort Street to vehicular traffic. For 7 years no action was taken, even though the downtown area was declining as the center of retail activity. Traffic congestion, inadequate parking, and competition from suburban shopping centers continued to drain business from the downtown. When plans were announced in 1957 for the construction of

the giant Ala Moana complex, merchants feared a mass exodus by large retail establishments to the suburbs. In response to this threat the Downtown Improvement Association was formed in 1958. The association's first action was to have a master plan developed for the downtown, and its members raised $90,000 for this purpose. Master plans were provided by several different planning experts, and two different approaches emerged. This tended to confuse the direction of the project, and little was accomplished for a 6-year period.

A test was carried out in July, 1961, however, when Fort Street was closed for the Golden Harvest Celebration. A majority of merchants were happy with the results, and expected traffic jams did not occur. Similar events took place over the next year, and the merchants considered them successful.

In 1962, in an effort to achieve an acceptable master plan, the Downtown Improvement Association commissioned a new study. The consultant came up with a plan that provided a third approach to the downtown, resulting in more controversy.

By 1963 the downtown merchants were feeling the effects of the opening of the Ala Moana Center, and their sales dropped from $64 million, or 15 percent of the city's total, to $55 million, or 9 percent of the total.

Eventually, after the City Planning Commission presented still another approach to the downtown in 1965, the firm of Victor Gruen Associates was commissioned in 1966 to develop a plan. The firm carried out an urban design study which showed that a mall on Fort Street would be desirable. The plan called for the downtown to be divided into a series of superblocks within which a system of pedestrian malls would be developed.

In January, 1968, the City Council approved the mall after 75 percent of adjoining owners indicated their consent, and $2.4 million was budgeted for construction.

Two parcels of land were purchased along Fort Street, one at King Street and the other, owned by Our Lady of Peace Cathedral, at Beretania Street. This land was needed to create a larger plaza at each end of the mall. New buildings such as the Bank of Hawaii were then set back from the mall.

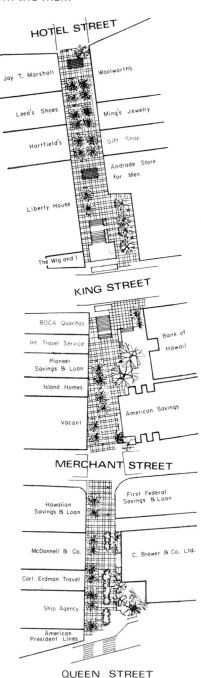

Design Features

ART The mall's major art work is a huge petroglyph mural 70 × 9 feet, cast in concrete and containing several hundred reproductions of ancient Hawaiian rock carvings. The mural is located in the King Street underpass.

The underpass was originally intended to accommodate all pedestrian circulation across King Street, but the city was petitioned by handicapped citizens to keep the on-grade crossing open.

CONCRETE ARCHWAYS The archways were designed to act as trellises and support flowering vines.

Sitting areas are provided between the archways, and many people eat their lunch there.

PAVING The paving is concrete with brick bands in a rectilinear design.

PLANTS Plant material includes a double row of false olive trees defining a central circulation path through the center of the mall.

Other trees, such as coco palms, coral trees, bottle brush, shower trees, and monkey-pod trees, as well as numerous flowers and plants, are used for accents.

NIGHT LIGHTING Lighting is placed on concrete piers in support trellises, as well as in planter boxes, and there are other fixtures at the underpass. A sound system is included in the overhead lighting fixtures.

FINANCIAL PLAZA Also adjacent to the mall, between King

View of mall from
King Street
underpass.

(*Opposite page*)
**Plan of three blocks
of the mall from
Queen Street to
Hotel Street.
(Photographs
courtesy of Gruen
Associates.)**

and Merchant Streets, is the new Financial Plaza, containing the Bank of Hawaii Building, American Savings and Loan Building, and the Castle and Cooke Building. The construction cost of this project was $17 million, and it was completed in 1969.

In Retrospect

Since completion of the mall, the decline of sales in the stores has stopped. When the mall was completed, new buildings worth $59 million were under construction. Several high rise office buildings in the downtown were constructed, and two major condominium apartment projects adjacent to the head of the mall were built. All major retail stores along the mall have remained.

Also, in 1971 Fort Street was privately extended one short block between Queen Street and Nimitz Highway to link with the AMFAC office buildings. This has improved pedestrian circulation.

View of concrete archway, lighting, and planting.

View of sitting area.

Fulton Mall

FRESNO, CALIFORNIA
Architects
VICTOR GRUEN ASSOCIATES
Landscape Architects
ECKBO, DEAN, AND WILLIAMS

Description
Fulton Mall is located in Fresno, California, a city with a population of 165,972. Fresno is part of the St. Joaquin Valley between Los Angeles and San Francisco. The mall is six blocks in length and creates a pedestrian area free of automobile traffic. Traffic is banned also from two streets crossing the mall, providing pedestrians with 0.5 mile of uninterrupted walks.

The mall features concrete paving with red pebbled bands, fountains, reflecting pools, arbors, sitting areas, children's play areas, sculpture, night lighting, and adjacent parking facilities.

The project was accomplished by creating an assessment district and by using Federal Urban Renewal Agency funds. The mall, which cost $1.6 million, was dedicated in September, 1964.

Development Strategy
The primary purpose of the mall was to revitalize the downtown, beginning with Fulton Street, a traditional shopping street congested with traffic.

In 1956 Sears, Roebuck moved out of the downtown to a suburban location. This action spurred

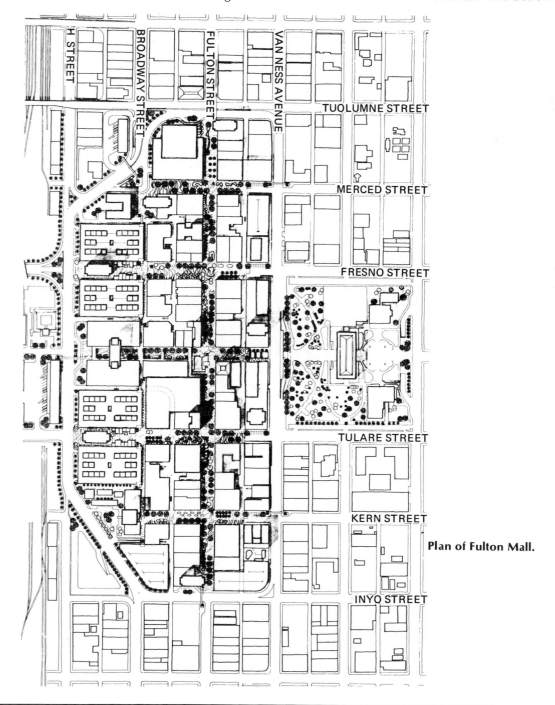

Plan of Fulton Mall.

merchants to take the initiative to improve the retail district.

The Fresno Redevelopment Agency was created in 1956. The Fresno Hundred Percenters, now called the Downtown Association, provided an organization of businessmen and property owners supporting renewal. In 1958 the city, the Redevelopment Agency, and the Downtown Association hired a planning consultant.

Planning the mall and overall superblock of 85 acres involved many groups. Among them were the California Highway Department, the county, the Civic Center Committee, the Convention Bureau, bus lines, the Trucking Association, the League of Women Voters, the American Institute of Architects, and federal agencies, as well as the city government.

To finance the mall, the Pedestrian Mall Act of 1960 was enacted by the state legislature. This act enabled main streets in commercial areas to be restricted and improved for pedestrian use. Costs of development could be assessed against the lands benefited or could be financed with other funds available to the city, including urban renewal funds.

Planning Considerations

The major planning objectives for revitalizing the retail district were the following:

1. To treat the center city as a core superblock that is pedestrian oriented.

Overall view of mall, showing paving and other features.

2. To provide peripheral parking in multistory garages surrounding the superblock.
3. To study freeway routes and circulation around core areas.

Design Features

FREEWAY ROUTES Freeway routes were established 20 years ahead of their construction, and the triangular freeway system was designed to provide a loop around the 2000-acre core.

PAVING The paving is formed of concrete with curvilinear bands of red pebbles imported from Mexico. The concrete was sandblasted and treated with an epoxy coating.

FOUNTAINS The mall was designed with many water features, including cascades, pools, and jets. Sculptures are also part of some of the fountains.

PLANTING Plant materials include 162 trees and 19,000 plants, giving much variety.

The trees provide canopies of shade along the mall.

SITTING AREAS Seating is provided on benches, as well as under trellised areas and around fountains, for many people.

SCULPTURE Sculpture has been provided by a citizens' group, which has raised over $150,000 for works of art. These art objects are numerous throughout the mall. An element that serves as a landmark is a large sculptural clock toward the center of the mall (see p. 64).

View of mall. (Photographs courtesy of Gruen Associates.)

MALL LIGHTING Lighting is provided by round globes on metal standards. Some outdoor cafes and children's play areas are also features of the design which add a variety of activities.

In Retrospect

The mall and 323 parking spaces were completed as the first step in renewing the downtown. In 1971 another 3000 parking spaces were added. Many building facades were rehabilitated, and the mall gained a national reputation for its planning and design.

When the mall was completed, it also appeared to be a success financially; it drew 57 percent of the retail market, up about 9 percent in retail sales. By 1971, however, after the opening of a second major shopping center in the suburbs, sales leveled off to 49 percent of the market.

Fountain with coping for sitting.

Stone sculpture.

Metal sculpture.

Fountain with back-drop of planting.

Granville Mall

VANCOUVER, BRITISH COLUMBIA, CANADA

Architects
BAIN, BURROUGHS, HANSON, AND RAIMET

Description

Granville Mall is a transit mall located in Vancouver, British Columbia, a city of 426,502 residents. It was planned to facilitate pedestrian use in a six-block (3000-feet) area along Granville Street from Nelson to Hastings.

Granville Street, which had six lanes of traffic with 1200 vehicles per hour, was reduced to two lanes of traffic with 100 buses per hour. Pedestrian walks were widened to as much as 35 feet, hundreds of large trees were planted, new paving was installed, and incandescent street lights were added in the first phase. In the second phase, sitting areas, bus shelters, and additional lighting were added.

The transit mall was accomplished with funds from assessment of property owners, the Federal Winter Works Program, British Columbia Hydro, and the city. Phase One was completed in August, 1974, and Phase Two in September, 1976. The cost of the project was $3 million.

Development Strategy

The primary purpose of the mall was to revitalize Granville Street, which was rapidly deteriorating. The design was to facilitate pedestrian use and act as a framework for redevelopment, along with creating a safer, quieter environment for people to enjoy shopping, business, theatres, and walking.

Granville Street was always an important street, with its theatre row, banking, small shops, and department stores. By the latter 1960s, however, shoppers seemed to have abandoned the narrow sidewalks and noisy streets for shopping

centers. The situation deteriorated until merchants petitioned the City Council to take action, and in the summer of 1972 a series of meetings was held between the city's Social Planning Department and police force and people concerned about Granville.

It was decided that, because of Granville's historical importance and its role as a gateway to the downtown, it was important to provide a long-term solution to the various social, business, and environmental problems of the street. A special joint committee made up of both city staff and City Council was established to study the feasibility of a mall. It was thought that a transit mall would be best. There were several reasons why the merchants wanted buses to be kept on the street. The primary reason was that access to stores would be maintained and that buses would encourage pedestrian flow. If a new transit system is installed, buses can be removed to make the mall completely pedestrian oriented.

The prototype for the Granville Mall was the Nicollet Mall in Minneapolis, which the city's task force on mall feasibility visited in August, 1973.

On September 25, 1973, the City Council approved the mall design by the consulting architect. A tight deadline of 12 months was set for Phase One, and methods had to be worked out to adhere to the schedule.

Policies relating to street vending, cafes, signs, loading, and street use were also determined.

Funding for the mall was as follows: property owners, $900,000; the Federal Winter Works Program, $543,000; British Columbia Hydro, $165,000; and the city, $1,338,560.

SIGNS Although many other cities with malls have tried to discourage or prohibit projecting signs, this change is not contemplated for

the Granville Mall. The Sign Bylaw was used to encourage awnings and canopies; other bright projecting signs, including theatre marquees, were allowed to continue in order to maintain some of the character that had developed on the street.

ZONING Zoning was amended to make the street more pleasant for pedestrians and to stop deterioration. Banks and financial institutions were limited to 25 feet of frontage on the mall because of the dead space often created by nonretail facilities. Massage parlors were controlled by making them conditional use areas that must be approved by the Development Permit Board.

STREET VENDING A Street Vending Bylaw was enacted, providing for licenses to be issued for specific locations distributed along the mall. Permits were issued to encourage a variety of goods on the mall. Special vendors' kiosks were also designed.

CAFES A set of simple guidelines was prepared to encourage the development of sidewalk cafes by restaurant owners.

CITIZEN PARTICIPATION No association concerned with Granville Street existed before the mall was constructed. First, an interim committee of merchants from each of the six blocks was appointed. This group then held elections and became the Granville Business Association. Through its membership fees, the association has developed programming events on the mall. During the summer of 1975, many cultural events were scheduled, including a series of "Mozart on the Mall" concerts, art and photographic exhibits, and puppet shows.

Design Features

In the first phase of development, basic elements such as trees, paving, and lighting were installed. The second phase included sitting areas, additional lighting, bus shelters, and other amenities.

PLANTING Tree-lined streets are an important feature in Vancouver. Therefore trees became the major focus and unifying element of the design and are used to define entrances to streets, to give a sense of separation of pedestrian areas from the transitway, and to create spaces for special activities. Over 200 trees, many of them with trunks 4 to 5 inches in caliper, were used on the mall. Beech trees were planted in the greatest number, with red maple, European ash, purple leaf birch, western hemlock, dogwood, vine maple, Oregon grape, and Scotch pine trees also used.

STREET LIGHTING Incandescent street lighting on early Vancouver lamp standards provides a feeling of warmth. There are also two lights at the base of each tree, along with outlets for special use. These outlets can be used to connect Christmas decorations.

SEATING Raised concrete and wood benches are arranged in groups around trees.

PAVING Paving is a light-colored exposed aggregate concrete.

CAFES Restaurant owners are granted permission to set up Parisian-style sidewalk cafes, with canopies and glass enclosures for inclement weather.

OTHER FURNISHINGS These include bus shelters and specially designed vendors' kiosks.

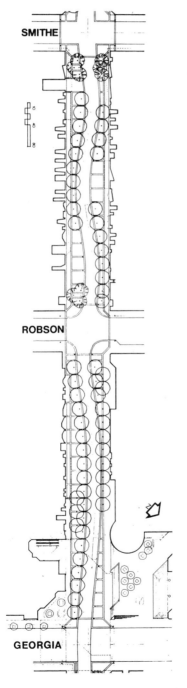

Plan of typical blocks on mall. (Photographs courtesy of Bain, Burroughs, Hanson, and Raimet.)

View of mall looking southwest from the corner of Georgia and Granville.

In Retrospect

In 1975 the assessed rental value of properties along the mall increased by about $636,000 over 1974 figures. A business tax revenue gain of over $60,000 (8 percent) was realized in 1975.

The mall's performance was particularly impressive in the 900 block, in which the rate of decay was worst before construction. Assessed rental values increased 50 percent from $300,000 in 1974 to $450,000 in 1975. This generated business tax revenues of $43,021, an increase of $14,250 for the block. In 1975 the assessed rental value for the 900 block of Granville, $452,850, equaled the revenue of the 1000 block of Robson Street, a most prestigious block.

In a survey of sales in January, 1975, 58 percent of the merchants said sales had risen over the same period in the previous year, and 73 percent attributed the improvement to the mall.

There have also been fewer complaints about crime on the mall.

View looking northeast from the lower end of mall. Winding streets provide a variety of pedestrian spaces.

Sitting area at corner of Georgia and Granville.

Detail of sitting area
and lighting for
tree.

View of bus shelter.

View of vendor's
kiosk.

Hamilton Mall

ALLENTOWN, PENNSYLVANIA

Architects, Engineers, and Landscape Architects

COPE, LINDER, AND WALMSLEY

Description

Hamilton Mall is located in Allentown, Pennsylvania, a city of 109,572 people, about 55 miles north of Philadelphia. Hamilton Street, the major downtown shopping street, has been turned into a semimall four blocks in length. Hamilton Street previously had five lanes of traffic, but has been narrowed to a roadway width of 22 feet. Automobiles, buses, and taxicabs can use this semimall. The semimall was developed to preserve and revitalize the central business district.

Hamilton Mall features an extensive cantilevered canopy system on both sides of the street, stretching the length of the mall and unifying its design. The mall also features new paving, lighting, traffic signalization, fountains, planting, kiosks, sitting areas, and heated bus stops. Within easy walking distance of the mall are 7500 parking spaces.

Activities on the mall include fashion shows, arts and crafts festivals, sidewalk sales, and Pennsylvania Dutch Day.

The semimall was funded by the Pennsylvania Department of Community Affairs and the city of Allentown. Construction was completed in November, 1973, at a cost of $5 million.

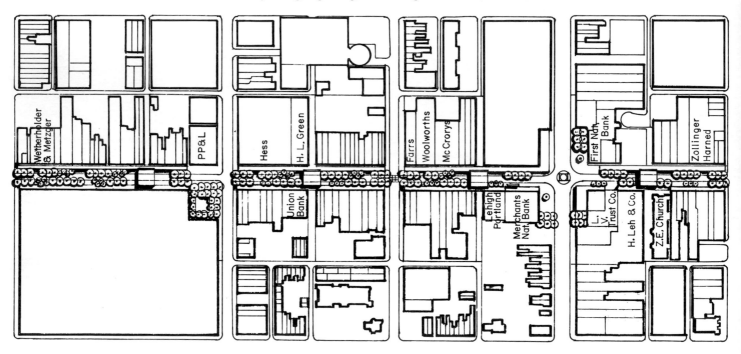

Plan of mall.

Development Strategy

In the mid-1960s the downtown was beginning to show signs of deterioration, with falling receipts and a dwindling tax base. Local merchants and public officials decided that a major study of the entire central city area should be made.

In April, 1967, a planning firm was retained to begin the center city study. The Progressive Center City Allentown Organization paid $15,000 toward the first study. Represented in the group were merchants, financial institutions, utilities, and private corporations. The city and state also helped fund the study, which reviewed such areas as traffic flow, markets, and treatment of residential areas in the center city.

The study, which was completed in February, 1969, recommended that a mall be developed on Hamilton Street and that residential areas surrounding the downtown be rehabilitated.

Design work on the mall began, and in February, 1972, construction started. The mall was to be completed by the Christmas season of 1973.

The Pennsylvania Department of Community Affairs provided $2.5 million of the funding, with the city of Allentown matching this with $2.5 million of general obligation bonds, for a total of $5 million. The Allentown Redevelopment Authority coordinated the overall planning for the project.

Design Features

CANOPIES The canopy system unifies the entire mall. There are 4800 linear feet of steel and Plexiglas in the cantilevered canopies. They provide some weather protection and have heating elements in gutters and downspouts to melt snow and ice. The canopy system is 14 feet high along walks and 12.5 feet wide. A 1-foot transition space between the canopy and existing buildings causes some problems at entrances to buildings in rainy weather.

The canopy continues across intersections and increases in height above the street.

LIGHTING Lighting is incorporated in the canopy system: 3000 incandescent lamps in round lexan globes line both the inside and the outside of the structure. Additional lighting is used at midblock, where metal halide lamps on high poles emit a brighter and more efficient light on the scene below. Along both sides of the roadway, 240 bollards 3 feet high with built-in lighting also help illuminate the area used by vehicles.

PAVING Hamilton Street originally had 12-foot-wide sidewalks. These have been widened to 29 feet and are paved with brick and concrete. The roadway through the mall has bituminous paving, but there is a concrete surface on drop-

Canopy covering brick sidewalk. (Photograph courtesy of Rohm and Haas Company.)

off areas, which are used for passenger and merchandise pickup.

RAISED PLANTERS Sixty planters made of concrete are used on the mall for trees, shrubs, and flowers.

PLANTING The mall has 130 trees, many of them red oaks planted directly in the walk areas with tree grates used around them.

The trees and grates are integrated into the paving design. Other planting includes shrubs, ground cover, and flowers.

FOUNTAINS The mall also features several fountains with aerated jets of water. Some of these are surrounded by low concrete walls similar to the planters.

OTHER FURNISHINGS Kiosks are also part of the street furnishings. They are surfaced with porcelain enamel to limit graffiti (see p. 59).

Sitting areas, heated bus stops, and traffic signals have also been designed for the mall. In addition, new utility lines have been placed beneath the center of the roadway as part of the mall construction, to limit disturbance to the mall in the future.

In Retrospect

Hamilton Mall was developed to provide a safe, attractive, easily accessible shopping area. The original idea of a full mall was abandoned when a test period that was to last for 90 days was stopped

View of canopy across width of street.

View of bollards and sidewalk areas.

after 1 week because of complaints from merchants.

The semimall concept has already spurred investment of over $30 million in new buildings, additions, and parking structures. The tax base has been improved and sales have increased, vacancies are down and employment is up. The mall is considered successful, is noted for its design, and is used by the entire Allentown community. Its first year of operation resulted in a sense of renewed vitality in the downtown.

View of paving and planters.

Ithaca Commons

ITHACA, NEW YORK

Architect
ANTON J. EGNER AND
ASSOCIATES

Landscape Architect
MARVIN ADLEMAN

Description
Ithaca Commons is located in
Ithaca, New York, a city with a
population of 26,226. The mall
establishes a pedestrian plaza for
two blocks on State Street and one
block on Tioga Street. The mall is
66 feet wide and 1100 feet
long.

The mall features a fountain,
covered pavilions, a children's play
area, a small amphitheatre area, sitting areas, raised planters, paving
of concrete and brick, bicycle
parking, planting of deciduous
and evergreen trees, shrubs, and
flowers, and night lighting. Building
facades along the mall have also
been improved, and parking
facilities adjacent to the mall added.

The total cost was about $1.13
million, with 85 percent provided by
private property owners and 15
percent by the city. The mall was
completed in August, 1975.

Development Strategy
The mall concept was presented in
1958 by the Greater Ithaca Planning
Board in response to deterioration
of the downtown. In the early 1960s
two urban renewal plans indicated
that the mall concept was important
to this goal, but no progress was

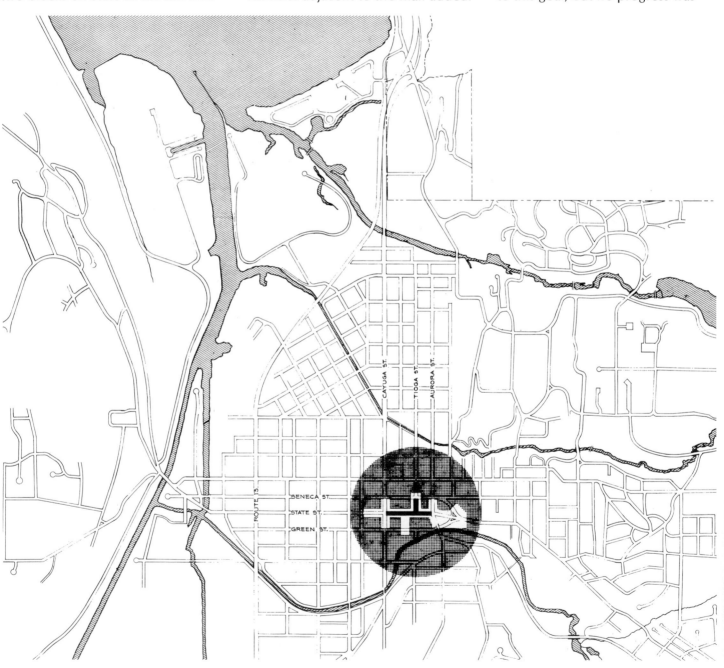

made until January, 1972. At that time a Citizens Action Committee for a Downtown Mall was appointed by the mayor. The committee included representatives from the Downtown Businessmen's and Businesswomen's Associations and the Area Beautification Council. Each business owner on the proposed mall was spoken to personally. In addition, a public hearing was held in March, 1973, to hear questions from representatives of community members.

In June, 1973, the Action Committee grew into the Mall Steering Committee, and additional members were added, including other merchants, the mayor, the planning director, and members from the Planning Board and Common Council. This committee was then responsible for the planning and development of the mall.

A traffic study was carried out, and data showed that from a traffic standpoint the mall was feasible. The city then committed itself to

providing 900 additional parking spaces in two structures adjacent to the mall.

When a survey of merchants made in 1973 indicated that 80 percent supported the mall idea, the decision to proceed was made. About 5 percent of the merchants opposed the project, but when one business sought a court injunction to stop construction, the city won the case. The mall involved no federal funds but required an amendment to New York State's Local Finance Law to

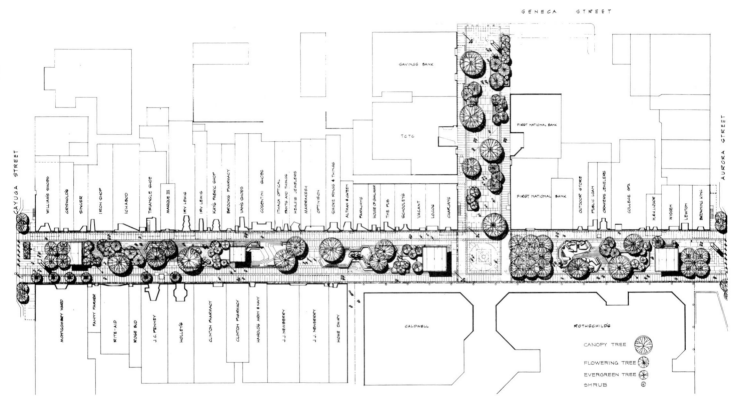

Plan of mall.

(*Opposite page*)
Mall in relation to downtown context. (Photographs courtesy of Anton J. Egner and Associates.)

permit 20-year bonding. In order to tax the property owners, a benefit assessment district was established. There are both a primary and a secondary district. The primary district fronts on the mall, and the secondary district taxes properties within 250 feet of the mall. The tax on properties in the secondary district decreases with their distance from the end points of the mall as measured from the centerline of their frontage.

Construction on the mall was started in June, 1974. In December, 1974, the mayor appointed a nine-person advisory board to set guidelines for common activities and to make recommendations for improvements to adjacent buildings. The board formulated an ordinance to regulate common activities, which was adopted by the Common Council on May 7, 1975.

The advisory board also had a Commons Design Advisory Team. This organization contacted all owners and merchants about improvement of their buildings. Buildings have been sandblasted or painted, false fronts on second stories removed, and signs improved.

Design Features

The design concept for the mall stresses flexibility to allow a wide variety of activities, both planned and spontaneous.

FOUNTAIN One of the features of the mall is a fountain with elements made of granite. The fountain also acts as a sculpture and symbo-

View of State Street before the mall was developed.

lizes a typical gorge in New York State, where streams flow over bedrock and provide a waterfall effect.

CHILDREN'S PLAY AREA The play area has wooden play structures, sliding boards, a chinning bar, and poles to slide down set in pea gravel in a space defined by walls and paving with a backdrop of pine trees.

PAVING Paving of major circulation paths is concrete with brick used in major activity areas. A brick band is also placed along the low sitting walls and is expanded into the niches where benches are set back from the main walks. Ramps for the handicapped are also part of the paving design of the mall.

RAISED PLANTERS Planters with concrete walls define activity areas, some having benches integrated into the planters. The height of the planter walls also allows casual seating throughout the mall.

COVERED PAVILIONS Pavilions on the mall provide weather protection and shade. These structures have wooden frameworks with metal roofs that are supported by round concrete columns.

NIGHT LIGHTING Lighting is placed on tall metal standards with other accent lighting used for feature elements. The overhead luminaires use sodium lamps.

PLANTING Plant materials used on the mall fall into five categories: canopy trees, trees used as sculptural or focal elements, small or flowering trees, evergreen trees, and evergreen shrubs. Trees include

View of fountain.

The children's play
area is a very
popular feature on
the mall.

Sitting area defined
by raised planters.

CENTRAL CITY MALLS

View of mall, show-
ing paving, raised
walls, and seating.

the Halka honey locust, Bradford pear, Washington hawthorn, Radiant crabapple, and red pine. The pine trees provide a backdrop for sitting areas, enclosure, windbreaks, and green color during bleak winter months.

The evergreen shrubs include compact Pfitzer juniper and dense Japanese yews. Flowers are also provided for seasonal color and are well maintained. They are planted in the raised planters throughout the mall.

In Retrospect

Since completion of the mall, sales have increased for most merchants in the mall by as much as 22 percent. The facade program, in conjunction with a sign ordinance, has been successful, and there has been a great deal of new construction in the downtown. The mall has also received recognition for its design. In addition, parking structures adjacent to the mall have been developed. These provide 900 parking spaces with free parking for the first 45 minutes and a nominal charge of 10 cents for the next 3 hours, which may be paid for by validation from merchants. Parking is heavily subsidized and was funded by the New York State Urban Development Corporation.

Pavilion on the commons.

CENTRAL CITY MALLS

Main Street Mall

CHARLOTTESVILLE, VIRGINIA

Landscape Architects
LAWRENCE HALPRIN AND ASSOCIATES

Economic Potentials
HAMMER, SILER, GEORGE, AND ASSOCIATES

Description
The Main Street Mall is located in Charlottesville, Virginia, a city with a population of 38,880. Charlottesville has a unique historic back-ground, being the home of Thomas Jefferson.

The mall, five blocks in length and 60 feet in width, is the main activity center of the central business district. It was therefore the best place to start downtown revitalization with the expectation that people will use the downtown if it is a pleasant place to be: visually attractive, clean, safe, and auto-free. Design features of the mall include new paving, lighting, fountains, kiosks, seating, and planting.

The mall was funded from the city capital improvement budget for 75 percent of its cost and from assessments of abutting property owners for 25 percent. The mall was completed in July, 1976, at a cost of $2 million.

Development Strategy
The idea of a mall began in 1971, when the city government decided that some action was needed to protect the tax base in the central business district. A Central City

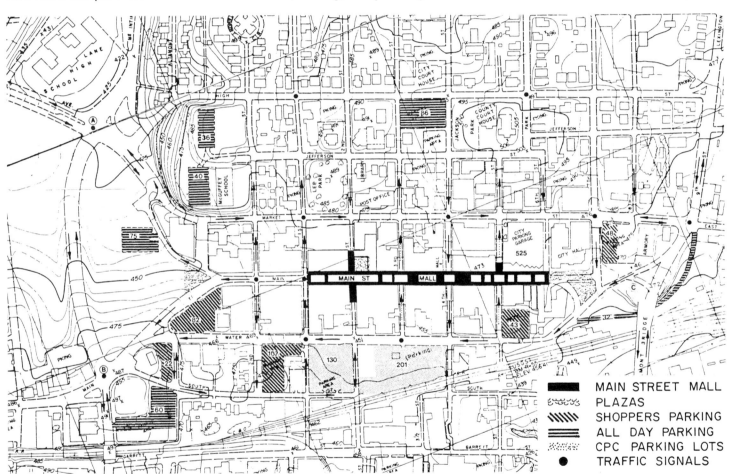

Location plan of mall.

Commission made up of area residents, business people, government officials, and others was formed to determine a concept for revitalizing the downtown. Their idea was a mall.

After the design consultant was retained, a 3-day workshop involving the Central City Commission was held. Thirty-two people participated. Some of the objectives agreed on were the following:

1. There should be pedestrian areas separated from automobiles.

2. Downtown amenities should be as good as those found in the best suburban shopping centers, or better.

3. The downtown should have many cultural and recreational features such as art, sculpture, music, and theatre.

4. Existing older buildings should be recycled and given new uses.

5. The architectural and historic character of downtown Charlottesville should be revitalized.

6. There should be as little vehicular traffic as possible crossing the mall.

7. There should be preservation and conservation of older structures on Main Street.

8. Design control and review provisions for downtown Charlottesville should be created and enforced.

After public hearings and a great deal of public controversy, the City Council voted to proceed with funds for the mall. The above objectives were then carried out.

Brick paving on the mall.

View of granite fountain.

Design Features

The design of the mall does not emphasize the linear quality of the street but instead reorganizes it into a series of outdoor rooms. These rooms which develop in a sequence of spaces, are defined by bosques of trees numbering six to eight in double rows.

PAVING The mall is paved in brick with concrete bands. Where intersecting streets have been closed off, concrete pavers form a pattern in the brick paving.

FOUNTAINS These features are made of granite and provide differing water effects. Three fountains are located on the mall. Two of them are small and have water bubbling out of granite blocks in sitting areas located beneath bosques of trees. The other larger fountain forms a focus on the mall, and has granite elements with water pouring into a metal container.

FLOWER POTS These elements, planted with junipers and flowers, add color throughout the mall.

KIOSKS Kiosks are also used on the mall and are lighted for night effect. The kiosks contain drinking fountains.

SITTING AREAS Sitting areas with benches are provided throughout the mall. These movable benches are located beneath bosques of trees adjacent to the large fountain.

LIGHTING Black metal poles with pendular clusters of four luminaires line the mall. Uplighting is also provided for trees.

View of main fountain.

PLANTING Trees are planted in groups to define spaces and to provide shade. The trees used on the mall are willow oak and maple.

In Retrospect

The mall creates a pleasant place for a variety of activities. Shaded sitting areas, especially those with fountains, create an inviting environment for people to relax, and benches can be arranged for ease of conversation.

(*Opposite page, top left*)
Kiosk on the mall.

(*Opposite page, top right*)
Seating on the mall is very flexible, and people can group the benches for ease of conversation.

View of granite fountain and sitting area.

Flower pots.

**Lights designed for
the mall reflect
incandescent light.**

**Bosques of willow
oaks are used on
the mall.**

Michigan Mall

BATTLE CREEK, MICHIGAN
Landscape Architects
JOHNSON, JOHNSON, AND ROY, INC.

Traffic Planners
HARLAND BARTHOLOMEW

Description
Michigan Mall is located in Battle Creek, Michigan, a city with 38,931 residents, 100 miles west of Detroit.

The mall was developed to revitalize the downtown shopping area. Michigan Mall covers four blocks, including one cross block at Madison Street. It stretches along the city's primary artery from Carlyle Street to City Hall at Division Street.

The right-of-way is generally 72 feet. The three blocks at the center of the mall are completely closed to traffic, and the blocks at either end are of the semimall type.

The mall features fountains, sculp-

ture, overhead trellis areas, new paving, a clock tower, display areas, lighting, sitting areas, and planting. The Michigan Mall was funded by special assessment, the city, and a private grant. The mall was completed in June, 1975, at a cost of $2 million.

Development Strategy
In 1959 the concept of a mall was discussed by the merchants in Battle Creek. The merchants considered urban renewal but decided not to

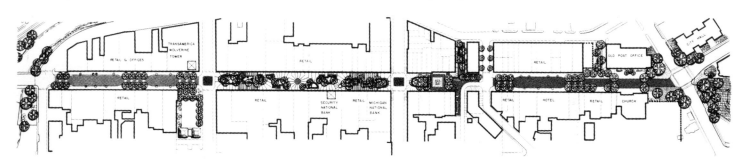

(Above)
Plan of the mall. (Photograph courtesy of Planning Department of Battle Creek.)

(Below)
Plan of a typical block. (Photograph courtesy of Planning Department of Battle Creek.)

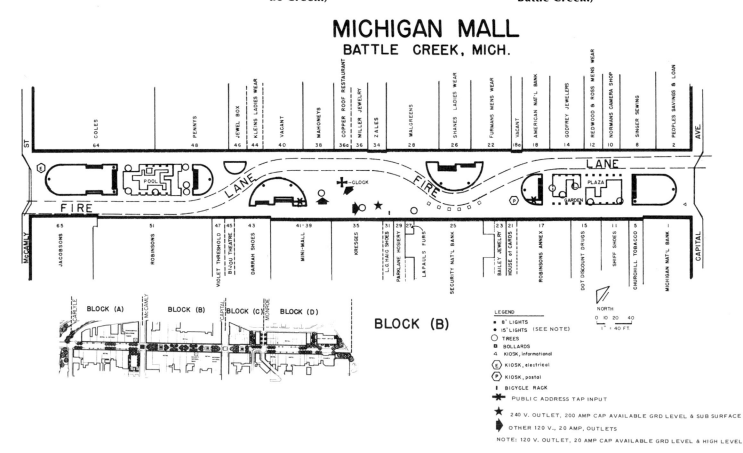

pursue this method for revitalization of the downtown. Funding from the Department of Housing and Urban Development was applied for but was not granted. Eventually, the Association of Retail Businessmen hired a design consultant to develop a plan for the downtown.

This plan was funded by a special assessment of the 250 businesses for 45 percent of its cost, by the city for 45 percent, and by a private grant from the Miller Foundation for 10 percent.

Design Features

The design concept allows for easy pedestrian circulation from one side of the street to the other and the relation of commercial or civic functions to the spaces created.

FOUNTAINS The plaza facing Civic Theatre has a fountain-sculpture as a focal point.

There is also a water feature plaza with a sunken pool and bubbler fountain.

PAVING The paving on the mall is brick and concrete.

CLOCK TOWER The major display plaza has a central clock tower built on a concrete structure.

TRELLIS There is a garden display plaza which has an overhead trellis area. Gas lighting is used in this area.

SITTING AREA There are several types of sitting areas. Some benches are built into raised planters or walls, while others are free standing.

RAISED PLANTERS Planters help define many of the spaces and form

Fountain with sculpture. (Photographs courtesy of Johnson, Johnson, and Roy, Inc.)

the edge of fountains and other features. They are made of concrete.

LIGHTING Night lighting in some areas is provided by gas-lit fixtures. In other areas metal standards with luminaires are used.

PLANTING A variety of trees and other plant materials is used on the mall, such as red maple, Marshall's seedless ash, redbud, cotoneaster, yews, azaleas, and flowers. The plant materials were selected for ecological compatibility with minimum maintenance.

In Retrospect
Sales of major stores increased up to 30 percent after the first year that the mall had been opened. Pedestrian traffic has also substantially increased.

Clock tower.

Trellis area with
concrete piers.

Fountain with bub-
bler.

Mid-America Mall

MEMPHIS, TENNESSEE

Architects
GASSNER, NATHAN, BROWNE

Landscape Architects
OLIPHANT AND ASSOCIATES

Engineers
ELLERS, REAVES, FANNING, AND
OAKLEY

Graphic Design
RINALDI AND ASSOCIATES

Description

Mid-America Mall is located on
Main Street in Memphis, Tennessee,
a city with a population of 623,530
residents. The mall stretches 12
blocks (4000 feet) from Exchange
Street south to McCall Street. The
mall is completely pedestrian
oriented for about 3000 feet from
Exchange Street to Union Street,
where a semimall begins. Although
there is generally an 85-foot right-
of-way along the mall, several areas
expand in width, particularly at City
Hall. In this location the mall links
the Convention Center and auditorium to the principal shopping area.
Another large space exists between
Jefferson and Madison Streets.
The mall features fountains, pools,
sculpture, sitting areas, planting,
pavilions, kiosks, banners, and
performance platforms.
The project was funded by a special
tax assessment of property owners.
Construction was completed in
December, 1976, at a cost of $6.7
million.

Development Strategy

The mall was developed to revitalize
the central city shopping area. The
Downtown Association, an organization of businessmen, was instrumental in promoting the mall.
Speakers were invited to give talks
on urban design, and several field
trips were taken to places such as
Atlanta and Minneapolis to see what

other cities were doing. A feasibility
study funded jointly by the city,
county, and businessmen was then
carried out by a planning firm.
The mall was to be the first step of a
total development plan.
Funding for the mall was achieved
by creating an assessment district.
The city provided funding on an
interim basis until money from the
assessment was available.

Design Features

The mall has been designed to be
pleasant for shopping and strolling.
It is, in effect, a linear urban park.
All physical features are placed to
create a 25-foot lane through the
mall for emergency access.

FOUNTAINS AND SCULPTURE
A long reflecting pool leads by
means of a ramp into the Civic
Center. A round fountain, 120 feet
in diameter with a 60-foot plume of
water, is the focus of the Civic
Center, which includes City Hall.
There is also a block-long water display which mixes sculpture and
fountains in the area from Monroe
to Union. Three smaller fountains
are located at Jefferson, Madison,
and Gayoso Streets. A welded steel
stabile is also located on the mall.

PAVING Materials used for the
paving pattern include aggregate
concrete, brick, and granite. Tree
grates are also part of the paving
design. Along the semimall, traffic
lanes are paved with brick and are
slightly depressed below the walk
surface. Bollards, along with planting, are used to distinguish cross
street areas.

PLANTING Trees are an
important design element on the
mall. They are used to reinforce the
auditorium space adjacent to the
reflecting pool, to provide shaded
sitting areas, and to distinguish
intersection areas at cross streets.
The trees used are ginkgo, locust,
linden, and sycamore.

KIOSKS AND PAVILIONS Each
block of the mall features a group-

ing of kiosks and pavilions to provide services such as concessions,
flower stands, ticket booths,
newsstands, postage machines,
and directories.
Canopies provide shelter for
persons waiting for the free tram, an
added convenience for shoppers.

PERFORMANCE PLATFORMS A
performance platform is located at
West Court and Main Street. The
Court Square area is the large space
between Jefferson and Madison.
Other small platforms are also
placed on the mall for speakers,
musicians, and impromptu per-
formances.

In Retrospect

Mid-America Mall provides a 12-
block environment to which many
amenities have been added.
Numerous activities may take place
in this revitalized area.

(*Opposite page*)
Plan of mall.
(Photographs cour-
tesy of Gassner,
Nathan, Partners.)

Stabile entitled "Apogee" by Louis R. Pounders.

View of mall paving and lighting.

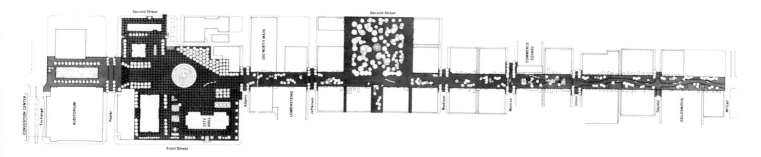

Nicollet Mall

MINNEAPOLIS, MINNESOTA

Planners

BARTON ASCHMAN ASSOCIATES, INC.

Landscape Architects

LAWRENCE HALPRIN ASSOCIATES

Description

Nicollet Mall is located on Nicollet Avenue, the main street of the shopping district in downtown Minneapolis, a city with a population of 434,400. The first phase of the mall was eight blocks (3200 feet) in length with an 80-foot right-of-way. An additional four blocks were added in the second phase.

Nicollet Mall is a transit mall with traffic limited to buses, taxicabs, and minibuses, which carry shoppers the length of the shopping district for $0.10.

The mall has a curvilinear or sepentine alignment, with a road width of 24 feet. The alignment provides changing motion and a variety of views as one progresses through the mall. The sizes of spaces also change, with some pedestrian areas as wide as 36 feet. The mall has four fountains, several sculptures, special clocks, a weather station, specially designed incandescent lights, and places to sit. Street furnishings have been designed to act as unifying elements for the mall. Additional elements such as bus shelters, a self-service post office, kiosks, traffic signals, paving, flower pots, and bollards have also been provided, as well as snow melting equipment.

The mall has a strong visual terminus to the north at Washington Avenue: the Northwestern National Life Insurance Building.

The project was accomplished by funds from an Urban Mass Transportation demonstration grant, an Urban Beautification grant, and a bond issue, to be redeemed by assessments of property located within 330 feet of the mall. The first eight blocks of the mall were completed in November, 1967, at a cost of $3.875 million.

Development Strategy

In the mid-1950s Nicollet Avenue was the prime shopping area of the downtown. Shopping centers were under development in suburban areas, however, and positive-thinking individuals formed the Downtown Council in 1955 to improve, expand, and enhance this shopping area. Council members included officers of major corporations, merchants, bankers, property owners, utility companies, and media representatives.

A new planning director was hired, and comprehensive planning, along with a study of the Nicollet area, was begun. The Downtown Council formed a temporary Nicollet Avenue Survey Committee in May, 1957. The committee decided that if Nicollet Avenue was improved the impact would be positive throughout the whole downtown. The concept of improving the street was then given high priority by the Downtown Council.

A permanent committee for Nicollet Avenue was formed, and planning consultants were retained to develop a report on the principles and techniques for retail improvement of the street. The report was completed in 1960 and showed that environmental improvement for the street was desirable.

The Planning objectives were as follows:

1. To improve pedestrian circulation.
2. To improve access and encourage mass transportation.
3. To strengthen the identity and image of Nicollet Avenue, thereby creating new opportunities for retail promotion.
4. To encourage private investment by creating a stable environment for retail sales.
5. To develop a transit mall of high aesthetic quality that would link neighborhoods with Nicollet Avenue. All bus routes were to use the mall, cross the mall, or be within one block of the mall.

In 1962 the Downtown Council adopted a plan for the mall which was approved by the City Council and the County Board of Commissioners. The Minneapolis legislature passed legislation to permit restriction of vehicles on the street and to allow assessment of property owners to help fund the mall.

The final assessment plan allotted more than half the total assessment to owners fronting on the mall, while properties off the mall to a distance of 330 feet accounted for the rest. Two benefit zones on the mall and off covered 18 blocks, with each zone having sections providing 100, 100 to 75, 75 to 50, and 50 percent allocations of the cost. The properties closest to the center of the mall paid the greatest proportion of both construction and maintenance expenses. The assessment district provided $2,751,785; the Urban Mass Transportation grant, $512,000; and the Urban Beautification grant, $483,500. Private utility companies cooperated by agreeing to check their lines and update them as necessary so that disturbance to the street in the future would be minimal. Utility costs were $2.5 million.

When the bid for construction of the mall came in high, the city decided to act as general contractor for the project.

Design Features

The mall is of high quality and has elegant detailing. Durable materials are used such as granite, brick, bronze, and copper.

Street furnishings are coordinated to provide unity in the overall design, and each block has its own features.

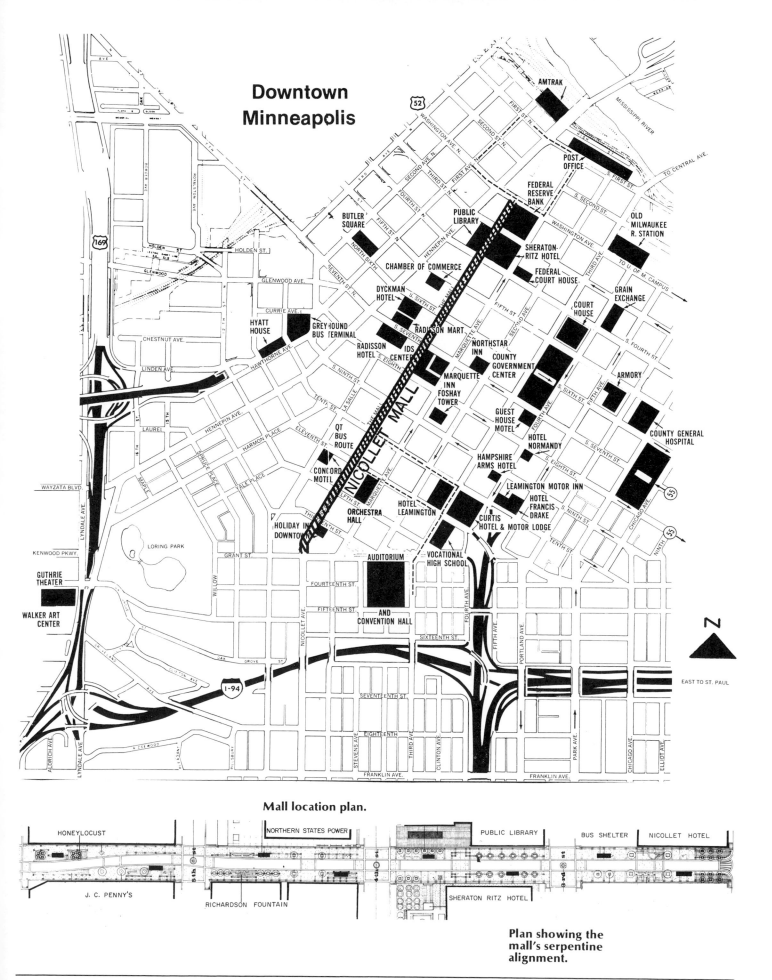

Downtown
Minneapolis

Mall location plan.

HONEYLOCUST NORTHERN STATES POWER PUBLIC LIBRARY BUS SHELTER NICOLLET HOTEL

J. C. PENNY'S RICHARDSON FOUNTAIN SHERATON RITZ HOTEL

**Plan showing the
mall's serpentine
alignment.**

FOUNTAINS The mall has four types of fountains. One is made of gray granite and covers an area 12 feet wide × 32 feet long. It gives a sculptural effect with the use of water complementing it. Another type of fountain has a bowl effect with water flowing at the center.

SCULPTURE The mall featured an 18-foot Calder stabile donated to the city by Daton's department store. The sculpture was relocated due to new construction.

PAVING The paving on the mall is predominantly brick and aggregate concrete; however, granite is also used in sitting areas. A snow melting system is incorporated in the paving. Tree grates are part of the paving pattern. Seventy-five 3.5-foot-high granite bollards with chains between them are used on the mall (see p. 54).

RAISED PLANTERS Thirty-three concrete planters capped with granite have several shapes. There are 22 square planters 8 feet in diameter, 3 hexagonal planters 12 feet in diameter, 4 octagonal planters 8 feet in diameter, and 4 circular planters 7 feet in diameter. Trees are planted in these, as well as directly in the sidewalk areas. Eighty small concrete pots are also used for flowers, which add color in summer months. The pots are 38 inches in diameter and 18 inches deep.

PLANTING About 96 trees are planted along the mall. These include honey locust with a light,

Aerial view of Nicollet Mall. (Photograph courtesy of Downtown Council of Minneapolis.)

airy foliage, green ash, Redmond linden, and hackberry.

OTHER FOCAL ELEMENTS Included are two clocks, a weather station, kiosks, and a self-service post office. The weather station is 15 feet high and includes a weather vane and anemometer. Humidity, barometric pressure, wind speed, time, temperature, and precipitation are measured.

NIGHT LIGHTING Lighting on the mall has been carefully designed and acts as a unifying element at night. The 150 incandescent lights with clear acrylic hoods and clear traffic bulbs provide a warm glow. The use of both two- and four-globe types gives a feeling of movement through the mall and adds variety.

BUS SHELTERS There are 16 specially designed bus shelters on the mall, 2 on each block on alternate sides of the street. These are well designed and are heated for use in the winter by five infrared overhead heaters. Sections at each end also contain electrical switching gear and transformers.

In Retrospect

Nicollet Mall is regarded as very successful. Pedestrian traffic has increased, and there is less congestion. Retail sales have risen about 14 percent, with much benefit to smaller shops. There has also been more than $225 millon of new construction or rehabilitation along the mall. The IDS Center, a 57-story structure octagonal in shape, built at

View of mall, showing features of a typical block. (Photograph courtesy of Downtown Council of Minneapolis.)

a cost of $125 million, has 2.25 million square feet. Completed in 1973, it contains an office, hotel, bank, gallery, theatre, and underground parking.

The mall has also helped to strengthen other areas of the downtown. The impact of the mall has spread beyond its immediate area to improve the regional center and its environs, thereby gaining a national image.

A system of skyway links at the second-story level of buildings is being developed to form a second pedestrian system of special convenience for winter use. The system was initiated in 1962; by 1985, 76 skyways will connect 64 blocks.

Mall Extension to Loring Greenway

To the south the mall is being extended four blocks and will link with Loring Greenway. Loring Greenway, in turn, will link the Loring Park Development District with the Nicollet Mall. This development district is to provide 1800 new apartments and townhouses in a nine-block area.

Northeastern National Life Insurance Building

This building forms an important terminus for the mall along Washington Street.

Richardson fountain.

(*Above right*)
Weather station.

Raised tree planters with granite cap.

Self-service post office.

Pedestrian lighting.

IDS Center and skyway links in foreground. (Photograph courtesy of Downtown Council of Minneapolis.)

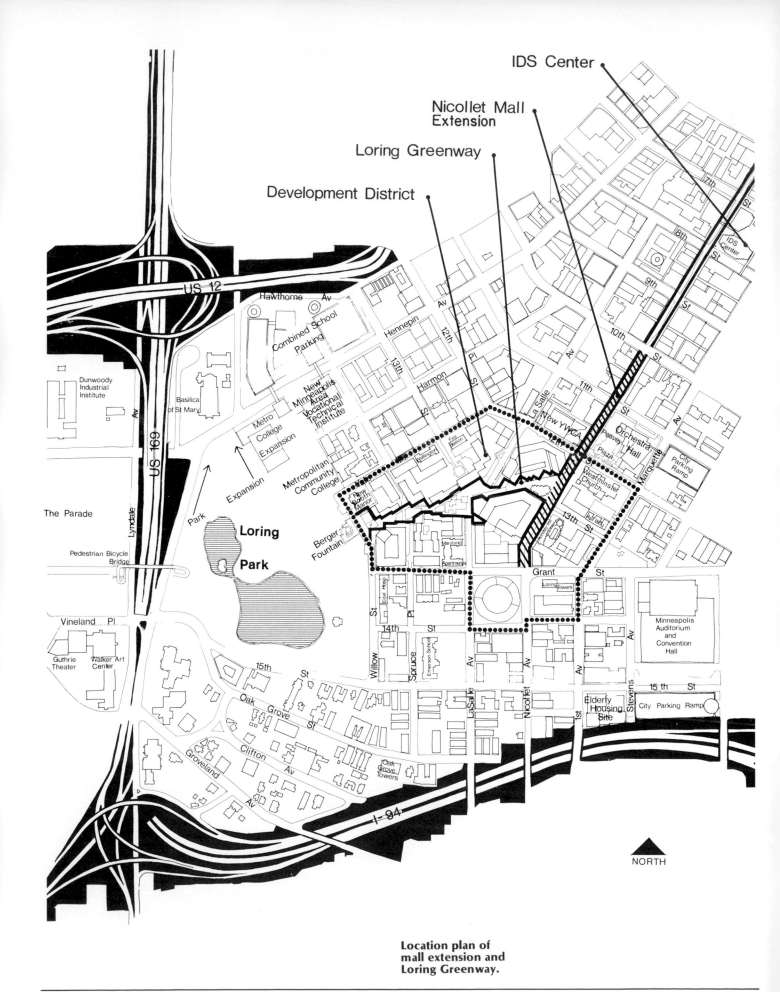

**Location plan of
mall extension and
Loring Greenway.**

Gateway fountain in foreground of insurance building.

Northeastern National Life Insurance Building.

Oldtown Mall

BALTIMORE, MARYLAND
Architects
O'MALLEY AND ASSOCIATES, INC.
Landscape Architect
WILLIAM H. POTTS

Description

Oldtown Mall is a full mall located in Baltimore, Maryland, a city with a population of 905,759. The Oldtown area is historically significant and is the site of one of the three original settlements that combined to become the city of Baltimore.

The mall is located on the 400 and 500 blocks of Gay Street for a length of about 1500 feet. The mall removes traffic from an area that was formerly choked with automobile and service trucks. Pedestrians had used narrow sidewalks and experienced difficult circulation on the crowded street.

The mall has a width of 45 feet and features a fountain, new brick paving, sitting areas, planting, and night lighting. Buildings along the mall have also been renovated as part of the renewal plan with the intention of recapturing the rich architectural qualities of these nineteenth century buildings.

Oldtown Mall was financed by Federal Urban Renewal Agency funds and Community Development Program block grant funds. The mall was completed in 1976 at a cost of $2.6 million.

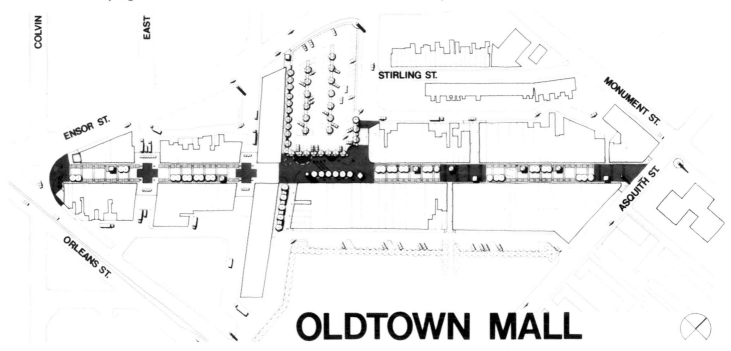

**Plan of mall.
(Photographs courtesy of O'Malley and Associates, Inc.)**

Development Strategy

The primary purpose of the mall was the revitalization of the Gay Street shopping area, which began to develop in 1813, when the Belair Market was established at the edge of town on Gay Street. In the 1880s this was the downtown of Baltimore. Since the 1940s the shopping area and residential neighborhoods gradually declined, and by 1960 Gay Street served low income black residents of public housing projects and adjacent neighborhoods picked for urban renewal. Assessed valuation dropped by 18 percent between 1963 and 1968, and more vacant stores and marginal businesses appeared.

Merchants petitioned assistance from the city and were included in an urban renewal program that comprised a project area of 35 blocks under the Department of Housing and Urban Development. In 1968 the Oldtown Project was initiated, and a tenuous alliance was formed between the black residential community, represented by a Model Cities Council, and the predominantly white merchants. The merchants appointed one member to represent it on the council. The city's community organizers and planners were important in maintaining the coalition. When special meetings were held with the merchants on rehabilitation standards, residents were always invited. Planning was carried out through biweekly community meetings over the period of 1 year.

The Oldtown Plan was adopted by the City Council through an ordinance that included mandatory rehabilitation standards. The plan called for the following:

1. Metered off-street parking areas in locations formerly occupied by commercial buildings.
2. Conversion of Gay Street into a shopping mall, and the rerouting of through traffic around the shopping area.
3. Mandatory rehabilitation of existing stores in accordance with city codes and special exterior standards. Financial assistance through HUD 312 loans was a major factor in securing the acceptance of rehabilitation requirements.
4. Redevelopment of the surrounding neighborhood for new housing, parks, and public facilities.

At the time the rehabilitation effort was to be started, the HUD 312 loan funds (3 percent for 20 years) were held up but eventually became available. Also, the Small Business Administration 502 Program was used.

The architectural consultant carried out a planning study to direct and assist the owners and tenants of commercial properties in the renovation program.

The renewal ordinance called for buildings to be restored to their original architectural character on upper floors. Flat signs on buildings are limited to the bottom of the second-story window or 13 feet above grade. Projecting signs may be no more than 7 feet beyond the building and no higher than 13 feet, or lower than 10 feet, above grade, with a maximum size of 4 square feet. Lettering identifying the business may be applied to ground floor show windows but may be no more than 2.5 inches in height.

Stores with new signs conforming to the sign control program and with newly renovated facades began to appear along Gay Street. After some merchants began their rehabilitation efforts, others followed, and nearly 100 percent of the owners cooperated, with the rehabilitation to be completed by the time the mall was opened.

The city's off-street parking commission provided metered lots on sites cleared through urban renewal. Although the low fees will probably not generate adequate funds to repay the cost of operation and debt service, the subsidy can be justified on the basis that taxes from stores are increased by the provision of parking spaces.

Design Features

FOUNTAIN In one area of the mall called Oldtown Square, several buildings have been removed and the mall has been widened to 70 feet. This area contains a fountain with adjacent sitting areas and is one of the focal points of the mall. The fountain has several aerated jets and an interesting texture on the base of washed river gravel set in concrete, surrounded by brick steps. This square also features a clock tower and performance area.

PAVING Paving is predominantly brick in different patterns, and in Oldtown Square circular concrete bands are used as part of the paving pattern in conjunction with round tree grates.

BENCHES Benches are made of concrete and are curved to act as sculptural elements.

PLANTING Trees are planted both in walk areas and in raised round redwood planters or tubs.

NIGHT LIGHTING The lights are clear round globes on metal poles at pedestrian scale, and there are also spotlights on higher poles to highlight various features of the mall.

In Retrospect

Along with development of the mall, storefronts have been rehabilitated with new signs conforming to the sign control program. Also, it appears that property values along the mall have increased since completion of the project. Black ownership of businesses has also increased from about 10 to 30 percent as a result of federal loan programs.

View of fountain.

**Brick paving with
circular tree grates.**

**Lighting and raised
redwood planters.**

Parkway Mall

NAPA, CALIFORNIA

Planners
HALL AND GOODHUE

Landscape Architects
SASAKI ASSOCIATES

Description

Parkway Mall is located in Napa, California, a city with 35,978 residents, located about 40 miles northeast of San Francisco.
A three-block (1000-foot) length is a full mall with a large plaza area 120 × 120 feet. Another portion is six blocks (2000 feet) long and is a semimall. The mall was developed to revitalize the downtown.
The mall features new paving, lighting, fountains, a clock tower, sitting areas, children's play areas, and planting.
Two new department stores have also been built in the downtown, and new zoning was approved to rezone out all peripheral, competing commercial areas to comply with the General Plan for the City of Napa and Environs.
The mall was funded by the Federal Neighborhood Development Program. The project was completed in August, 1974, at a cost of $1.5 million for the full mall and $8 million for the semimall.

Development Strategy

Planning studies go back to the mid-1940's, when a preliminary study was done for urban redevelopment in the central business district (CBD).
In 1952 a planning consultant prepared a master plan that was adopted by the City Council, but no action was taken regarding the CBD.
In August, 1959, an ad hoc group of citizens began a series of meetings to investigate urban renewal and gather information on methods of financing. Two years later, on August 30, 1961, this group of eight members was designated by the City Council as the Napa Urban Renewal Committee. The committee was enlarged to 28 members in May, 1962, and recommendations were given to the City Council to establish a redevelopment agency and begin negotiations with the Federal Urban Renewal Agency in order to begin a renewal plan.
In November, 1962, the City Council created the Napa Community Redevelopment Agency. Not much happened, however, until June, 1966, when a new planning director for the city was appointed.

The pace of action then began to pick up; a planning firm was retained, and by August, 1968, the General Plan for the City of Napa and Environs was approved by the Planning Commission and adopted by the City Council in November. Also, in November, 1968, "A Workable Program for Community Improvement for Napa" received certification by HUD.
In January, 1969, the City Council reactivated the Napa Community Redevelopment Agency, dormant

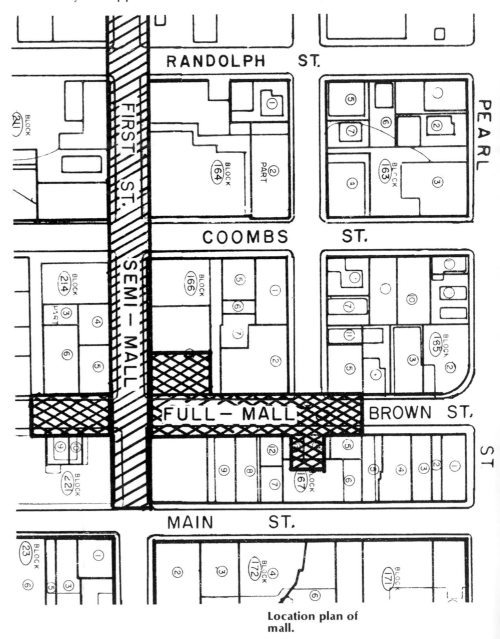

Location plan of mall.

since 1962. City council members became members of the agency, funds were applied for, and a public hearing was scheduled.

In December, 1969, the redevelopment plan was adopted by the City Council. Funds were approved by HUD in January, 1970, for the area called the Parkway Plaza Redevelopment. Construction got underway in 1971, with the reconstruction of one block on First Street from Coombs to Randolph. Three years later the entire mall was completed, along with two department stores and three off-street parking lots.

Design Features

The mall has many design features that have given the downtown a new vitality.

PAVING The mall is paved predominantly in brick with concrete bands.

LIGHTING Lights are clear round acrylic globes attached to wooden standards, to wooden trellis structures, and to a sculptural clock tower that acts as the focus of the large plaza area.

FOUNTAINS A fountain is also part of the plaza area and provides a waterfall effect, with water flowing over natural stone into a pool.

PLANTING Trees planted along the mall shade the sitting areas.

CHILDREN'S PLAY AREAS These areas have wooden play equipment and sliding boards.

OVERHEAD STRUCTURES A wooden trellis stretches throughout the full mall, providing shaded sit-

View of mall, showing clock tower, lighting, fountain, and paving. (Photographs courtesy of Sasaki Associates, Inc.)

ting areas and an interesting shadow pattern on the paving. Night lighting is incorporated into the structure.

OTHER STREET FURNISHINGS
These features include kiosks, bollards, raised planters, and other elements.

In Retrospect

Napa has become one of the first small cities in California to reverse the trend toward suburban shopping centers and downtown decay, to the extent of building two new department stores in its downtown. This was partially accomplished by zoning policies that restrict major commercial development to downtown Napa's 324-acre Parkway Plaza Project for both the community and the county. Some commercial property on the periphery of the downtown has been downzoned to residential. This restrictive zoning works in Napa because the concept generally has citizen support.

Night lighting effect.

Penn Square

READING, PENNSYLVANIA

Landscape Architects

THE DELTA GROUP

Description

Penn Square is located in Reading, Pennsylvania, a city with 84,097 residents, 60 miles northwest of Philadelphia. It is a pedestrian-oriented square in the 500 block of Penn Street that has been closed to through traffic. The 400 block has also been renovated and allows two lanes of traffic in each direction with drop-off areas for buses, taxis, and deliveries.

On the northeast end of the 500 block there is a convenience parking area for 18 cars and access to a service lane. The service lane is unique to this plan and allows deliveries to stores with no other access. Each block is about 530 feet long and 160 feet wide. The square features two cascading fountains, sitting areas, brick and concrete paving patterns, night lighting, extensive landscaping, and two sheltered bus stops on the 400 block.

The square was developed with funds from a variety of sources, including the Pennsylvania Department of Community Affairs, the city of Reading, Berks County, donations from local merchants, and a special tax assessment on Penn Square property owners. The Penn Square project was completed in May, 1975, at a cost of $1.6 million.

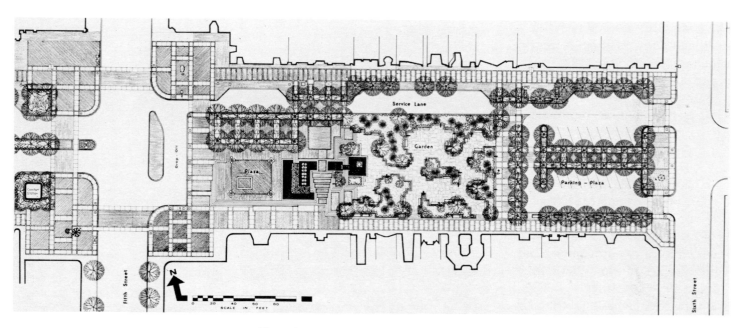

Plan of Penn Square.

Development Strategy

In 1969 local businessmen, with the support of the Chamber of Commerce and city government, began to look for possible improvements in downtown Reading. The Downtown Core Revitalization Committee of the Chamber of Commerce, working with an architect, proposed preliminary plans that were presented to the City Council.

In 1971 the mayor appointed the Mayor's Committee of 25 to spearhead the Penn Square Project. The committee worked with the Reading Redevelopment Authority, which was founded in 1952. This group was able to secure financial assistance as follows: the Pennsylvania Department of Community Affairs, $758,000; the city of Reading, $450,000; Berks County, $175,000; donations from local merchants, $90,000; and property owners in Penn Square, $180,000 in the form of a special tax assessment. In 1972 an architectural firm was retained to carry out planning and design studies for the square. In August, 1973, construction began. The City Council has established a seven-member Penn Square Commission to oversee the management of programs, promotions, and activities.

Building facades are also being restored, and signs and graphics controlled.

Design Features

The square has attracted shoppers, strollers, and office workers who bring their lunches to eat on benches and steps.

FOUNTAINS Two types of cascading fountains are located on the square. One is bowl shaped with water pouring from it, while the other fountain has 12 jets. The fountains have a capacity of 8000 gallons per minute, provided by three pumps.

GARDEN AREA Located toward the center of the plaza, a garden provides a quiet area offering many benches on which to relax. The garden is paved in flagstone and consists of a series of several spaces defined by plant beds.

PAVING Paving is in a brick and concrete pattern. The brick is red and reflects the architectural heritage of Reading. The concrete bands add rhythm and interest.

PLANTING There are 239 trees on the square. Deciduous trees such as oak, linden, and plane trees are used, along with evergreens, for example, hemlock, pine, and spruce. There are also shrubs such as rhododendron and azalea, as well as ground cover and bulbs.

NIGHT LIGHTING As part of the development, new street lights, low level bollard lights, walkway plaza lights, and landscape area lights have been used. The mercury vapor type was chosen.

FACILITIES FOR THE HANDI-CAPPED All public facilities are

View of fountain.

accessible to the handicapped. At each intersection, ramps have been provided in the paving system for the convenience of persons in wheelchairs.

PUBLIC STRUCTURES Two sheltered bus stops in the 400 block of Penn Street are provided, and a comfort station is planned in the future. A newsstand that also sells lottery tickets is located near Sixth Street.

In Retrospect

Penn Square forms an interesting framework in which a variety of activities take place. Throughout construction of the project most merchants maintained their former sales level or had increased sales. During construction there was a positive marketing approach with special events such as Lucky Sales Days. At present the majority of stores on the mall are doing quite well. The square has received design recognition and another block is presently being renovated adjacent to the mall.

Cascading effect of water.

Aerated jets of water provide a focus for the fountain, which is lighted for night effect.

Brick and concrete paving pattern provides rhythm in its design. Bollards with built-in lights and tree grates are also part of the design.

Plaza 8

SHEBOYGAN, WISCONSIN

Landscape Architects
LAWRENCE HALPRIN AND
ASSOCIATES

Planners
BARTON ASCHMAN ASSOCIATES

Description
Plaza 8, a full mall, is located on 8th
Street in Sheboygan, Wisconsin, a
city with a population of 50,000. The
mall, 3.5 blocks in length, stretches
from Ontario Avenue south past
New York Avenue. It is 1500 feet in
length with a right-of-way of 80 feet,
but widens to form a large plaza
adjacent to the library.

The purpose of the mall is to revitalize the downtown shopping area.
Pedestrian traffic and vehicular traffic have been separated, and convenient parking space has been provided.

Design features of the mall include
a fountain with a cascading effect,
new paving, lighting, planting, sitting areas, and other furnishings.
The mall was funded by the Federal
Urban Renewal Agency and by the
city. The project was completed in
July, 1976, at a cost of $1.6 million.

Development Strategy
Downtown Sheboygan has
experienced great pressures for
change. There was a gradual
deterioration of existing facilities
and services, along with declining
property and taxable values.

**View of mall.
(Photographs cour-
tesy of the
Sheboygan Depart-
ment of City
Development.)**

CENTRAL CITY MALLS

The overall objective of the mall is to return the downtown to a sound condition physically, functionally, and economically.

The Sheboygan Redevelopment Authority is the official agency responsible for the redevelopment of the downtown. The authority was created by the Common Council in 1966 and consists of seven appointed, unpaid commissioners, two aldermen, and five citizens.

A master plan developed in 1966 for the rebuilding of the downtown proposed a pedestrian plaza and the filing of an application for a Federal Urban Renewal Agency grant. In 1967 a large regional shopping center opened on the periphery of Sheboygan. This generated action by the city and the Chamber of Commerce, in a 50-50 financial partnership as they moved ahead into formal renewal planning. When the application reached HUD, the agency was impressed by the city's initiative and funded the first phase of the project.

The mall was submitted and approved by the Common Council in January, 1972. The federal government approved the project in July, 1972.

The project was funded for 75 percent of its $1.6 million cost by the Federal Urban Renewal Agency and for the remaining 25 percent by the city. The city's share will be paid through its provision of the new library and new parking facilities.

The design was developed to maintain and strengthen Sheboygan's competitive position as a regional and metropolitan shopping center. Functional, economic, and aesthetic values were introduced to complement modernized retailing methods.

The mall was also developed to reduce vehicular and pedestrian conflicts in the downtown shopping area. Short-term parking for shoppers is provided. This is convenient for those using the mall.

Design Features

PAVING The paving on the mall is predominantly brick. The alleys in the downtown are perpendicular to the main axis of the plaza and are paved with brick to extend the effect of the mall.

To provide a sense of continuity with the city's past, all of the old brick paving underlying the existing bituminous street that was excavated was carefully removed and cleaned. Forty thousand pavers were reused in low seating walls, brick edging, and the floor of the lowest and also largest reflecting pool at the bottom of the water feature.

FOUNTAIN An interesting water feature is located in the space adjacent to the library. The fountain is formed of concrete elements with water bubbling out of concrete blocks and then cascading down a series of lower blocks to echo one of the Indian definitions of the name "Sheboygan," originally meaning "place of rumbling waters."

View of mall paving, brick walls, lighting, and planting.

The fountain's waterfall has a drop of approximately 10 feet with a flow of 10,000 gallons per minute.

SEATING Wooden benches are placed adjacent to low brick walls forming planting islands.

LIGHTING Night lighting is provided by clear incandescent lamps with clear acrylic hoods at 12-foot height for pedestrian scale. There are also lights on high poles, which may be focused for more efficient illumination or used to emphasize special features.

PLANTING The plaza has approximately 230 evergreen, flowering, and shade trees and 180 flowering shrubs. Flowers are used for additional interest and color. As an additional feature at the southern end of the mall, a new municipal library was constructed and set back 50 feet to form a large planted space. The space is mounded 3 to 4 feet and planted with ash, oak, and birch trees to form a small forest in the downtown.

In Retrospect

The plaza represents one of the last large projects financed by the Federal Urban Renewal Agency. The plaza also has half-block extensions under construction at both the north and south ends.

Cascading water feature.

Portland Transit Mall

PORTLAND, OREGON

Architects
SKIDMORE, OWINGS, AND MERRILL

Landscape Architects
LAWRENCE HALPRIN AND ASSOCIATES

Engineers
MOFFATT, NICHOLS, AND BONNEY

Description
The Portland Transit Mall is located on 5th and 6th Avenues in downtown Portland, Oregon, a city with 379,967 residents. The mall is 11 blocks (2800 feet) in length on each avenue for a total of 22 blocks. The streets have an 80-foot right-of-way with each block 260 feet to the centerline of cross streets. The mall begins at Madison Street and proceeds north to Burnside. This transit mall has two bus lanes and one automobile lane in all but 6 of the 22 blocks. The purpose of the mall is to help eliminate automobiles from a major portion of the central business district by acting as the hub of a regional transit system. The project also assists in improving air quality by providing a 60 percent reduction of air pollutants in the downtown.

The mall features new paving, fountains, sculpture, kiosks, bus shelters, sitting areas, comfort stations, and traffic signalization.

The transit mall was funded by the Urban Mass Transportation Administration and by Tri-Met, the local transit agency. The project was completed in November, 1977, at a cost of $15 million.

Development Strategy
Before December, 1969, private carriers served Portland's mass transport needs. Between 1950 and 1970, however, a sizable decrease occurred in the number of commuters using mass transit. By 1960 persons using mass transit constituted only 19 percent of commuters, and by 1970 only 15 percent. Numerically, the decrease was from 45,000 in 1950 to 20,000 in 1970. Commuters, on the other hand, increased by 50,000.

In 1969 Tri-Met became the principal operator of the transit system. The city of Portland developed a downtown plan, announced in 1972, that called for a transit mall along 5th and 6th Avenues. The Portland City Planning Commission approved the mall concept, and the City Council endorsed it in January, 1972. This followed the Urban Mass Transportation Administration's approval for partial financing of a preliminary study of the mall. Tri-Met selected a team of consultants to develop a preliminary design. Several alternative designs were studied. The scheme chosen has two exclusive bus lanes through the mall with a third lane for automobile use in 16 of the 22 blocks. If volume of transit traffic increases as expected, the third lane will also be used for one of the following:

1. Buses in the third lane in the opposite direction.
2. Shuttles or special route buses.
3. Continuation of buses on the mall as originally planned.
4. Use of high capacity vehicles such as fixed guideway or light rail in the left lane.

The mall was funded by the Urban Mass Transportation Administration for 80 percent of its cost and by Tri-Met for the remainder.

Design Features
The mall was designed to be inviting to residents and visitors, to be beneficial to downtown businesses, and to encourage an alternative to the use of automobiles. Street furnishings were designed to be complementary in form and materials.

FOUNTAINS Six large fountains are placed at entrances to the mall at Burnside Street, on 5th and 6th, and between State and Washington, and Yamhill and Taylor, where the automobile lane is replaced by wider pedestrian areas.

PAVING The transit mall features a composition of textures, colors, and natural and man-made materials.

One material used is brick in a herringbone pattern on sidewalks and pedestrian zones. Brick also defines borders around trees, light standards, and intersections. Concrete is used in other areas, along with granite for curbs and gutters. Tree grates, also part of the pattern, are made of cast iron.

LIGHTING Some of Portland's old lighting standards are used to add a unique character and a continuity with the city's past. New crystal spheres replace the old globes. These lights have a 20-foot height. There is also low lighting in bollards at midblock.

PLANTING The planting design has 250 London plane trees along the avenues. At least six trees have been placed on each side of every block.

BENCHES Benches are at midblock locations. They have a double curve of wood slats banded with bronzed metal at the center and ends. The benches face in two directions perpendicular to the street.

BOLLARDS Granite bollards connected by bronzed chains are placed at each intersection. They indicate to pedestrians where the mall begins and guide them to crossings.

KIOSKS AND CONCESSION BOOTHS Communication, display, and small merchandising facilities are placed along the mall. These provide places for announcements, exhibits, and refreshments, and to ease in use of the mall. The concession booths, of two sizes, are used for the sale of flowers, newspapers, and snacks.

SIGNALS AND SIGNS New 13.5-foot-high traffic signals are also used on the mall. They have bronze-colored metal supports and illuminated graphics. In addition, there are police and fire call boxes on the mall.

CLOCKS Clocks are placed on the old lamp standards. Four of these are used along the mall. Each clock has four faces and has a height of about 16 feet.

BUS SHELTERS These shelters are transparent pavilions con-structed of components similar to those used in the rest of the mall. For protection from wind and rain they are open only on the street side. Bronze-colored metal is used for the structural system.

In Retrospect

The Portland Transit Mall is one of the most extensive of its type. As a hub, the mall provides a convenient bus transfer point, serving as a link with suburban transit, shuttle buses, and intercity buses.

Lovejoy and Civic Center Forecourt Fountains

As part of the pedestrian circulation system, the mall is only a short distance from the Lovejoy and Civic Center Forecourt Fountains, a few blocks to the south. These fountains, especially the Civic Center Forecourt Fountain, are very spectacular and draw numerous people who enjoy watching them and participating in wading, sunbathing, and lounging. The fountains are built of concrete (see pp. 160, 161).

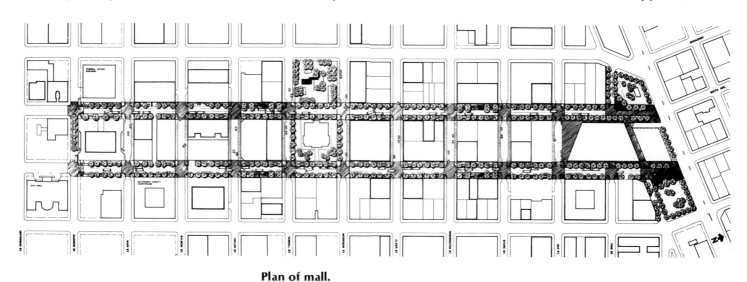

**Plan of mall.
(Photographs courtesy of Tri-Met.)**

Plan of a typical block.

**Night lighting of
partially completed
mall.**

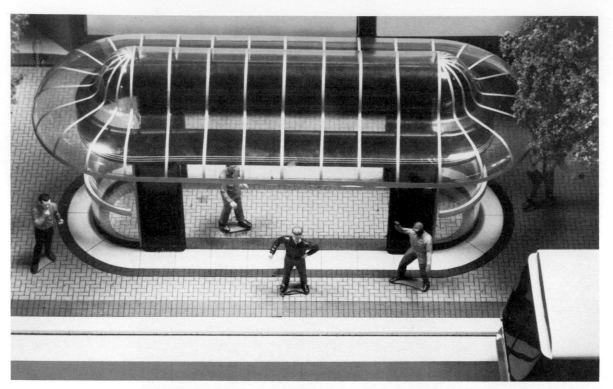

Model of typical
bus shelter.

Civic Center Fore-
court.

**View of Civic
Center Forecourt,
by Lawrence Hal-
prin.**

River City Mall

LOUISVILLE, KENTUCKY

Landscape Architects

JOHNSON, JOHNSON, AND ROY, INC.

Architects

RYAN ASSOCIATED ARCHITECTS

Description

River City Mall is located in downtown Louisville, Kentucky, a city with 361,706 residents in a county of 733,000. The mall forms a pedestrian area three blocks in length for 2700 feet along Fourth Street and has a width of 60 feet. Two cross streets, Chestnut and Walnut, penetrate the mall and had to be considered in the design to minimize pedestrian conflict with automobile traffic.

The mall features a circulation concept that encourages people to move from one side of the street to the other for ease of shopping. Toward the center of the mall special activities are located, including outdoor restaurants, children's play areas, sitting areas with fountains and sculpture, theatre-block plazas, planting, and night lighting.

The project was accomplished by assessment of affected property owners for $1.5 million and a HUD grant of $213,000. Mall construction began in July, 1972, and was completed in August, 1973.

Development Strategy

Fourth Street, chosen as the location of the mall, had once been the main commercial area of the downtown. It is presently located between the new riverfront project comprising a hotel, office buildings, and a large plaza, and the downtown core to the south.

The primary purpose of the mall was to revitalize this portion of the downtown. The Louisville Central Area, Inc., composed of 186 property owners, retailers, and financial leaders, met with the mayor, the county judge, the Board of Aldermen, utility companies, and the Louisville Departments of Traffic Engineering and Public Works to initiate the mall project in 1971. The preliminary design was funded by the Louisville Central Area, Inc. The objectives for the mall were as follows:

1. To help stop the decline of land and property values in downtown Louisville.
2. To create a better business climate.
3. To strengthen public confidence in the development of Louisville's downtown core.
4. To give the public a highly usable open space for its own enjoyment.

Design Features

River City Mall was designed as "A Place for People." Much attention has been given to human scale, and for those working downtown the mall offers relief from traffic and congestion. At lunchtime the mall is filled with people eating outdoors, meeting friends, and observing others.

FOUNTAINS Several special activity areas are located toward the center of the mall between circulation paths. Some of these places have sitting areas with fountains and sculpture and a canopy of trees to provide shade.

THEATRE-BLOCK PLAZAS These plazas provide places for band concerts.

PAVING Paving on the mall is a combination of concrete and brick. Concrete paving defines the major circulation path through the mall, while activity areas are paved with brick.

PLAYGROUNDS Small playground areas are also part of the design.

PLANTING Planting includes shade trees planted directly in the base plane of the mall with tree grates around them. Other plants are in raised planters and in pots. Some of the trees used are the sweet gum, oak, and southern magnolia.

NIGHT LIGHTING Lighting is at pedestrian level at a 12-foot height and provides uniform illumination for good safety conditions.

In Retrospect

In the months following completion of the River City Mall in 1973, sales in stores along the mall increased approximately 15 percent according to an information poll taken among the merchants. In 1974, however, the volume of sales decreased, corresponding to the national recession, and in 1975 sales remained constant.

In August, 1976, the assessed value of properties along the mall was reduced by 6.5 percent, based upon a decrease in revenues produced by the properties.

The mall has been a success with downtown users and is known for its unique design.

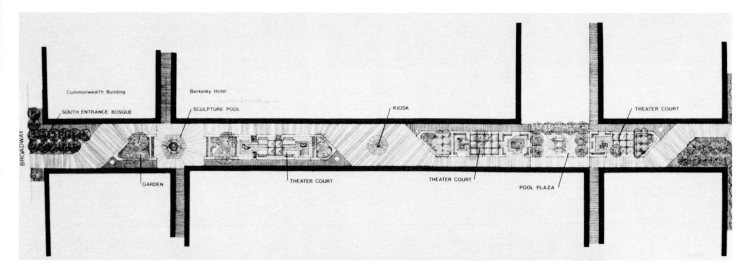

Plan of 600 block of mall. (Photographs courtesy of Johnson, Johnson, and Roy, Inc.)

Theatre-block area.

Sitting area with fountain.

Children's playground.

Paving and covered canopy area.

Planting and lighting.

Sparks Street Mall

OTTAWA, ONTARIO, CANADA

Architects

HELMER ASSOCIATES

Description

The Sparks Street Mall is located in Ottawa, Ontario, the Canadian capital, which has a population of 365,921. The mall forms a pedestrian area three blocks in length with a width of 60 feet.

At Elgin Street at the east end of Sparks Street, the mall connects with Confederation Square and is only one block from Parliament Hill to the north and a half block from the National Arts center along Elgin. The mall, which has been very successful, includes within its three blocks some of the most valuable properties in the city. More than $1 million in city taxes is collected in this area annually.

The mall features fountains, sculpture, kiosks, canopies, lighting, planting, sitting areas, and a small stage.

The Sparks Street Mall was funded by the city and by assessment of property owners. It was completed in 1967 at a cost of $636,000.

Development Strategy

In the late 1950s a well known town planner, Jacques Greber, suggested that Sparks Street might be a good location for a pedestrian mall. In September, 1959, the Ottawa Board of Trade took businessmen, civic, and government officials to see a pedestrian precinct in Toledo, Ohio. Some of the businessmen were enthusiastic about the concept and

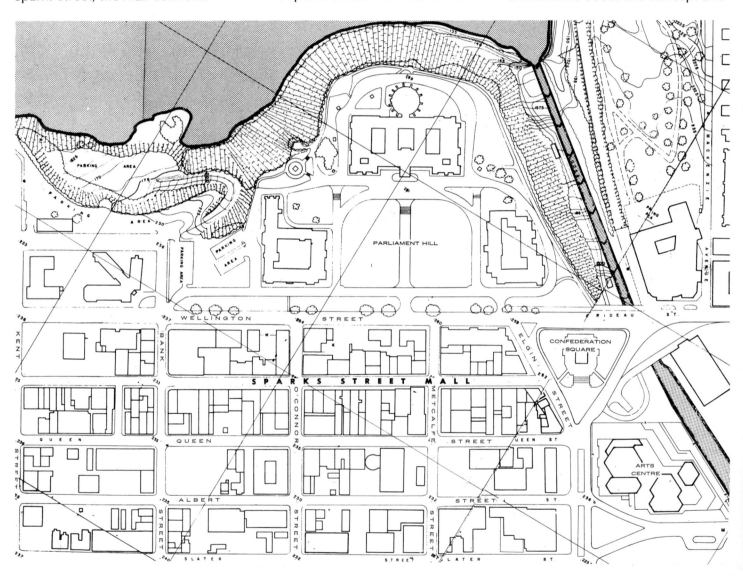

Location map.

formed the Sparks Street Development Association. The association wanted to create and test a mall on three blocks of Sparks Street. In early spring of 1960 the City Council agreed to approve necessary legislation and share the cost for a temporary mall up to a maximum of $15,000. The rest of the budget was to be raised by the merchant members of the Sparks Street Development Association. The mall was to open in May and be removed after Canada's Thanksgiving in October, 1960.

A research committee studied traffic flow, parking, and retail sales during the duration of the mall experiment. The research data showed that the mall was a success, and in 1961 a second summer mall was funded by the merchants.

After a third temporary mall was built in 1962, it was decided that a permanent mall should be developed, and a citizens' committee was formed. A report was then presented to the Board of Control in October, 1963.

City Hall was aware that the mall had the backing of the public and that deterioration of the downtown was about to lower tax revenues. The mall was therefore included in the 1965–1966 capital budget. The amount budgeted was $578,000, to be shared equally by the city and by owners abutting the mall. An amendment was inserted in enabling legislation so that the mall would proceed only if a majority of owners, representing one half of the assessment involved, consented. In October, 1965, Sparks Street owners offered to pay the cost to winterize another temporary mall, while the city provided snow removal. Consent was then obtained from more than 90 percent of the property owners, and approval to proceed was given by the Ontario Legislature in June, 1966.

A committee to provide for the welfare and maintenance of the mall was also proposed. This committee would be composed of two members from the City Council, two Sparks Street property owners, and two merchants.

Design Features

FOUNTAINS The mall features several fountains; one has stainless steel elements of varying heights forming a sculpture, along with aerated jets of water.

SCULPTURE An interesting sculpture in the form of abstract figures is adjacent to a sitting area toward Elgin Street.

PAVING The paving on the mall is concrete with an aggregate texture used around special features to add interest.

PLANTERS There are several different types of raised planters; some form small sitting areas and contain trees, shrubs, and flowers. Flowers in many different colors are used in raised planters throughout the mall.

Fountain with stainless steel elements.

NIGHT LIGHTING Overhead wiring has been placed underground. The mall lighting is at pedestrian scale on metal standards with round white globes. Both individual globes and clusters of four globes are used on the mall.

CANOPIES Canopies are in the form of free-standing elements that give shade to sitting areas.

OTHER ELEMENTS Also within the mall area are a small restaurant, a small raised stage area covered with an awning in summer months, and a clock that is a focal element near the Royal Bank of Canada.

In Retrospect

The mall has the advantage of separating heavy pedestrian movement on Sparks Street from relatively unnecessary but congested vehicular circulation. The mall has improved rerouted bus traffic flow and stimulated business on Sparks Street.

Pedestrians like the mall; it is a recreational area for people and a very busy place. The taxes are the highest in the city, and no vacancies remain since the area became a mall.

Also, some problems anticipated from the change in traffic routes have not been as severe as many people predicted and have not adversely affected the general traffic flow through the center of Ottawa. The mall is now being expanded an additional block to link with the Garden of Provinces. Much new development has also taken place

Sculpture of abstract figures.

Raised planters and built-in seating.

along the mall, including the Bank of Canada's new headquarters and several new office buildings.

National Arts Center

The mall is less than half a block from the National Arts Center on Elgin Street. The Arts Center has three theatres to accommodate 3563 patrons, a dining lounge, an indoor-outdoor cafe, a bookstore, and a large underground public garage. The National Arts Center is also adjacent to the Rideau Canal, which connects Ottawa with Kingston and the St. Lawrence River. The canal is 123.5 miles long, with 47 locks and 24 dams. Near the Arts Center the canal has a very urban character and with its pedestrian walks provides, in effect, an extension of the recreational activity provided by the mall.

Raised stage with awning.

Clock, as a focus.

Rideau Canal adjacent to National Arts Center.

Washington Square

LANSING, MICHIGAN

Landscape Architects

JOHNSON, JOHNSON, AND ROY, INC.

Description

Washington Square is located in Lansing, Michigan, a city with a population of 131,403 people. The mall creates a pedestrian plaza three blocks (1065 feet) in length along Washington Avenue and has a width of 115.5 feet. The first phase of the mall is bounded to the north by Shiawassee Street and to the south by Michigan Street. In the future the mall will be continued four more blocks south to Lenawee Street.

Streets cross the mall at each block, and at the Michigan Street entrance a bus stop and auto drop-off are located.

The mall features a spacious plaza in the 200 block of Washington Avenue for outdoor sales events and festivals; other parts have reflecting pools, sculpture, fountains, children's play areas, shaded sitting areas, and night lighting. The mall was accomplished with funds from the Federal Urban Renewal Agency and was completed in September, 1973, at a cost of $850,000.

Development Strategy

The primary objectives of revitalizing downtown Lansing were to improve the tax base and to stimulate business investment by creating

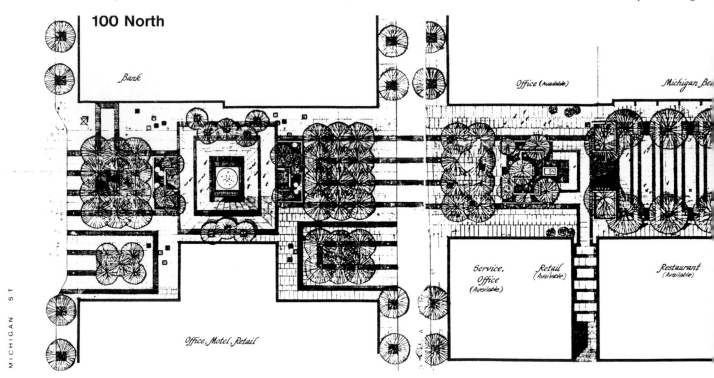

Overall plan of mall.

an inner city complex that would be convenient to use and pleasant to visit.

During the period from 1953 to 1964, tax revenues from parts of downtown Lansing dropped as much as 50 percent. There was a decline in business due to inadequate parking, deteriorating buildings, poor lighting, fire hazards, and a rising crime rate.

The mall was part of the Project One, Lansing Urban Renewal Program. Application was approved by HUD in 1963, and implementation for Project One began in February, 1965. Planning studies and a design for the mall were initiated in 1971 with completion of construction in 1973.

The plans provided that all buildings be oriented in design to use of the mall. Pedestrian passageways and plazas were designed to encourage easy pedestrian access to and from parking facilities and business establishments.

The renewal program also called for construction of five municipal parking structures to hold 4000 vehicles.

Design Features
FOUNTAINS AND SCULPTURE

The mall features pools, fountains, and sculpture.

A special sculpture called "Construction 150" serves as a gateway to the mall. It was developed for Lansing by artist Jose de Rivera at a cost of $90,000. Half the cost of the sculpture was financed by the National Endow-

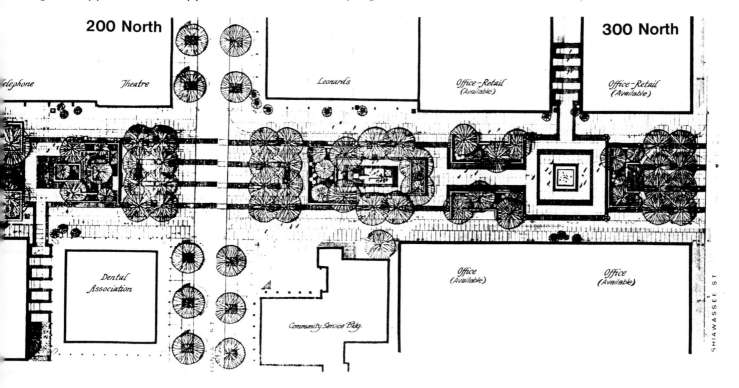

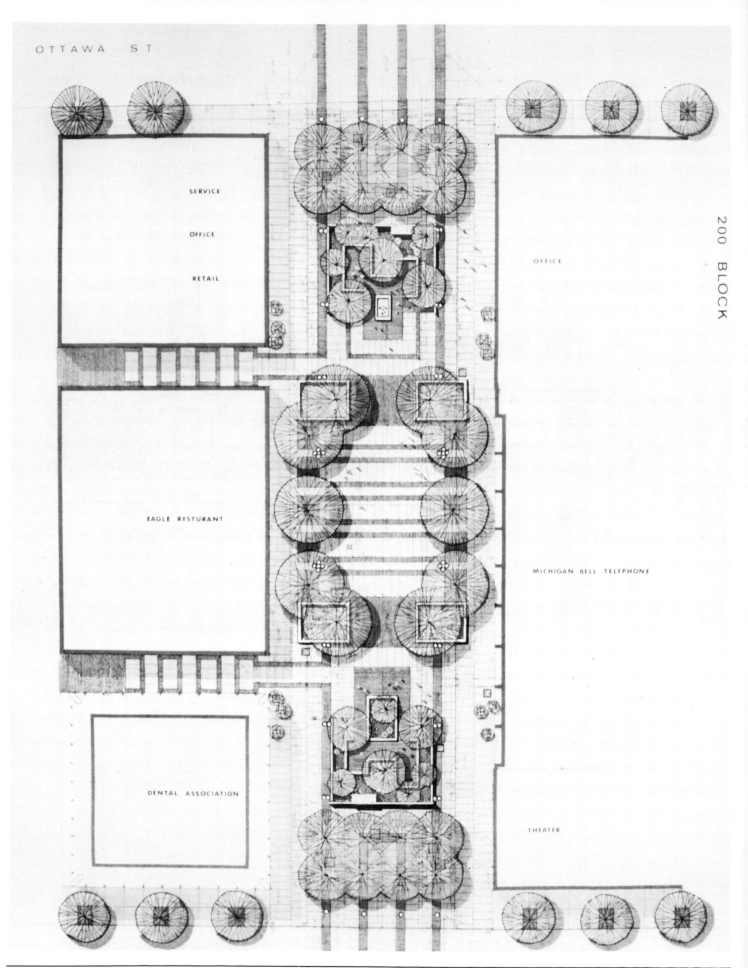

OTTAWA ST.

SERVICE

OFFICE

RETAIL

EAGLE RESTURANT

DENTAL ASSOCIATION

200 BLOCK

OFFICE

MICHIGAN BELL TELEPHONE

THEATER

ment for the Arts, with the remainder paid for by private contributions.

The mall has a sunken plaza with a pool and sculpture in the 100 block. Sitting areas and canopies of trees provide shade.

Toward the center of the mall, there is a spacious plaza with space for business displays, outdoor sales events, festivals, and special activities.

PLAY AREA AND EXHIBIT AREA

A play area and an exhibit area are located in the 300 block. In the center of the exhibit area is a reflecting pool, surrounded by paving on which canvas-covered display areas may be set up.

The children's play area has wood climbing structures, along with a slide, sandbox, and playhouse. The area is shaded by trees and has benches for viewers.

PAVING Paving is concrete with brick bands, larger activity areas having additional brick paving. The pattern provides rhythm.

KIOSKS Kiosks are part of the street furnishings and are located in two areas of the mall.

SEATING Seating is provided at strategic locations in the mall. It is placed away from main pedestrian circulation and directed toward interesting views, such as sculpture and planting.

PLANTING Plant materials have been carefully selected to provide shade and to filter views of vehicular traffic. Little-leaf lindens form canopies at entrances to the

Children's play area.

(Opposite page)
Plan of 200 block. (Photographs courtesy of Johnson, Johnson, and Roy, Inc.)

Outdoor concession.

square, while honey-locusts provide light shade for interior areas without obscuring views of other features. Smaller plants add color at different seasons of the year. Rhododendron, azaleas, pieris, bayberry, yews, ivy, and small trees such as the redbud and shadblow serviceberry are used.

NIGHT LIGHTING Lighting is provided by dual luminaires on tall standards, and pedestrian scale lighting by twin opaque plexiglass cylinders. Clusters of the cylinders simulating large candelabras are used in the larger open areas of the square.

Accent lighting is provided by low indirect fixtures, softly illuminating low walls, sculpture, and planting.

In Retrospect

Washington Square is an important first phase in Lansing's downtown redevelopment. The mall provides a variety of activities and will be expanded in the future.

View of kiosk.

(Above, left) **Sculpture and drinking fountain.**

Fountain and sitting area.

Wyoming Avenue Mini-Mall

SCRANTON, PENNSYLVANIA

Architects, Engineers, Planners and Landscape Architects

BELLANTE, CLAUSS, MILLER AND NOLAN

Description

Wyoming Avenue Mini-Mall is located in the 100 Block of Wyoming Avenue in downtown Scranton, Pennsylvania, a city of 103,564 residents. The mall was planned to facilitate pedestrian use along Wyoming Avenue where the two major department stores in the downtown are located. The mall is 650 feet in length and has a general width of 100 feet between opposite building facades.

Wyoming Avenue, which is a two-way street, had four lanes of traffic and two parking lanes. In the final semimall concept, on-street parking is removed and the street narrowed from 62 to 40 feet. This allows for much wider pedestrian walk areas and related amenities. Bus pull-off areas are also provided to facilitate transit use.

The mall has a clock tower, sculpture, children's play area, concrete brick pavers, and pedestrian walk lighting as well as street lighting with utility wires placed underground. Raised planters, seating, kiosks, new traffic poles, drinking fountains, flower pots, bollards, and much new planting are also provided.

View of mall.

The mall was funded by Community Development Program, Economic Development Administration funds, and private funds from the merchants in the 100 Block of Wyoming Avenue. The mall will be completed in 1979, at a construction cost of $862 thousand. Construction began on the project in May 1978, after some delay due to an extension to the project being considered.

Development Strategy

The primary purpose of the mall was to begin the revitalization of downtown Scranton, with the 100 Block of Wyoming as the first step in the process. This block was the most important single one in the Central Business District, accounting for about 60% of the tax base of the city. Two large department stores are located here along with several banks, a variety of shops, restaurants, and some offices.

Many plans and traffic studies had been done in the 1960s but little had been accomplished in the downtown until 1974, when some of the merchants on the 100 Block became interested in the idea of a mall. A design firm was contacted to develop feasibility studies on locating the mall in this block and alternate concepts for full and transit or semimalls. These plans were exhibited during a week when the 100 Block was closed to traffic during Downtown Shopping Days. Interest in the idea of a mall was generated, but controversy developed over what type of mall should be built, if the 100 Block was the place to begin, and if one block was enough for the first phase. During this period, funds from the Community Development Program were available but were not adequate to build a design having a canopy system. The merchants

decided on a mall without the canopy and on a two-lane curvilinear design that would allow buses on the mall during shopping hours and both cars and buses on the mall at all other times.

The merchants also agreed to assess themselves for $100,000 to show the city they were willing to contribute money toward the block on which they were located. The city then agreed to using $300,000 of Community Development Funds for the mall.

City Council approved the idea of the mall and passed an ordinance so that the street could be narrowed. This was approved on November 24, 1976.

An interesting event then occurred. To develop the mall properly, $1 million were needed. It became possible in 1977 to apply to the Economic Development Administration for the remaining funds needed. In order to accomplish this, the City Council had to approve the application for funding. On the first vote,

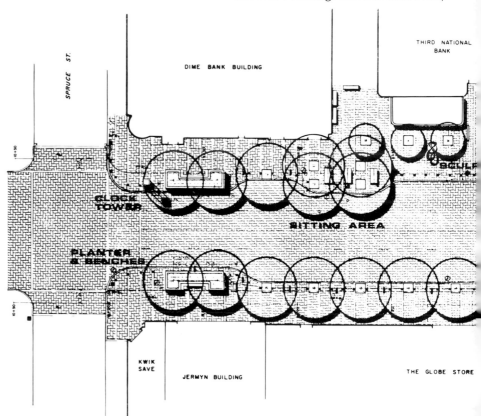

Plan of mall. (Photographs courtesy of Bellante, Clauss, Miller, and Nolan.)

March 23, 1977, City Council, by a 3 to 2 vote, vetoed the application because they were not convinced a mall was an answer to the city's needs for revitalization.

The merchants, news media, and public became very outspoken about the need for the mall as the first step in revitalizing the downtown, and after many newspaper and television editorials, and work by the merchants, Chamber of Commerce, the Mayor, and others, another Council meeting was held on discussion of the application for funding. The application for EDA funds was approved by a 3 to 2 vote on April 6, 1977.

After the project had been funded in August of 1977, and during development of final construction drawings, the major property owner on the 100 Block of Wyoming Avenue publicly objected to the two-lane scheme originally agreed upon, claiming there would be traffic problems. That claim was never substantiated, but wishing the revitalization of the block to move forward, the Mayor proposed a compromise solution to the merchants. This semimall removed the parking lanes and narrowed the street to 40 feet. It will be possible to narrow the street further to create a two-lane scheme or a full mall in the future.

While the majority of the merchants backed the two-lane plan, all agreed that for the project to proceed on schedule and to receive funding and eliminate possible lawsuits, the

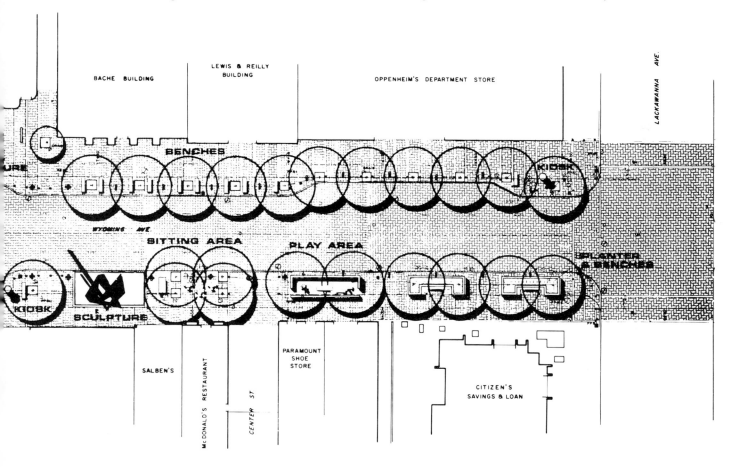

Mayor's proposal was the only feasible alternative. The project proceeded on this basis and approval from all parties was obtained.

Design Features

The mall has many design features that create an interesting environment in which to shop, stroll, eat lunch, and have special events.

PAVING The entire base plane of the mall is paved with concrete pavers. Walk areas are in a rustic colored concrete brick paver with aggregate concrete bands to give rhythm to the design. The roadway has granite curbs and is paved with a thicker concrete brick paver as are the crosswalk areas at Spruce and at Lackawanna Avenue.

The installation of interlocking concrete pavers and aggregate concrete pavers used for bands gives color, texture, and rhythm to the mall's paving design.

Three-foot high granite bollards provide interest and additional safety at bus drop-off areas.

SCULPTURE Two sculptures are proposed on the mall to act as feature elements and to provide cultural amenities in the downtown.

CLOCK TOWER A clock tower is provided near the intersection of Wyoming Avenue and Spruce Street. The clock has lighted faces that are for night time viewing.

KIOSKS Two kiosks are located on the mall. Both are of duranodic bronze aluminum and have night

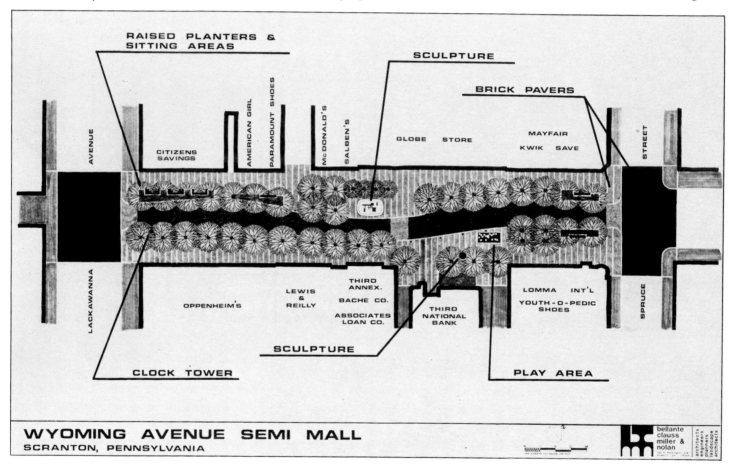

Preliminary plan of mall.

lighting. One serves as a directory while the other encloses electrical equipment.

PLAY AREA A small children's play area, provided with wood play equipment, is included so that all age groups can enjoy the mall.

INTERSECTION SIGNALIZATION Contemporary traffic signal structures will enhance the intersections at Spruce Street and Lackawanna Avenue. These have a bronze color and incorporate

pedestrian walk signals and police call boxes.

NIGHT LIGHTING Lighting is provided on 30-foot duranodic bronze aluminum poles for the roadway and on 12-foot high duranodic poles for pedestrian areas. Up-lights are used to illuminate the sculptures and trees in raised planters.

SEATING Double benches are provided facing in two directions for views along the mall as well as singly in other sitting areas. Seating

is also incorporated in raised concrete planters. Granite tables are available for eating or playing cards.

PLANTING Shade trees are used to form a canopy along both sides of the mall. London Plane trees were selected for their hardiness and interesting bark and are planted in both sidewalk areas and in raised planters. Evergreen shrubs are also planted in the raised planters as well as in some granite pots.

In Retrospect

The Wyoming Avenue Mini-Mall has acted as a catalyst for downtown revitalization. It has sparked an interest in the downtown and inspired those interested in improving it to work together. During this period of planning for the mall, a commission on architecture and urban design was approved by the Mayor and City Council at the request of an Ad Hoc Committee to help improve the aesthetics of the city and to encourage the use of up to 1% of funds for works of art on public projects.

The city is also reviewing ways of adding additional parking in the downtown which is badly needed. Funding for an extension of two additional blocks to the mall along Lackawanna Avenue is also being sought. Interest has also grown for renewing other blocks in the downtown area and both the city and merchants look forward to additional renovation in the future.

(Above)
Installation of pavers.

View of raised concrete planters with random board finish forming sitting areas.

Appendix

Catalogue of Central City Malls

Location	Population	Type	Name
Burbank, California	88,871	Full	Golden Mall
Fresno, California	165,972	Full	Fulton Mall
Napa, California	35,978	Full	Parkway Mall
		Semi	
Oxnard, California	71,225	Full	Park Plaza Mall
Pomona, California	87,384	Full and semi	Pomona Mall
Redding, California	16,659	Full	Redding Mall
Redlands, California	36,566	Full	Redlands Mall
Riverside, California	140,089	Full	Riverside Downtown Mall
Sacramento, California	257,105	Full	K Street Mall
Santa Monica, California	88,289	Full	Santa Monica Mall
New London, Connecticut	31,630	Semi	Captain's Walk
Wilmington, Delaware	85,000	Full	Market Street Mall
Washington, D.C.	756,510	Full	Library Place and
		Full	Gallery Place
Miami Beach, Florida	87,072	Full	Lincoln Road Mall
Tampa, Florida	297,586	Semi	Franklin Street Mall
Toccoa, Georgia	6,971	Full	Downtown Shopping Mall
Honolulu, Hawaii	324,871	Full	Fort Street Mall
Centralia, Illinois	15,217	Full	Centralia Downtown Mall
Danville, Illinois	42,570	Full	Vermilion Park
Decatur, Illinois	90,397	Semi	Landmark Mall
Freeport, Illinois	27,736	Full	Freeport Downtown Plaza
Rockford, Illinois	147,370	Full	Rockford Mall
Springfield, Illinois	91,753	Full	Old Capital Plaza
Evansville, Indiana	138,764	Full	Main Street Walkway
Michigan City, Indiana	39,369	Full	Franklin Square
Richmond, Indiana	43,999	Full	The Promenade
Burlington, Iowa	32,336	Full and semi	Jefferson Street Mall
Dubuque, Iowa	62,309	Full	Town Clock Plaza
Atchison, Kansas	12,565	Full	Downtown Mall
Kansas City, Kansas	168,213	Semi	Kansas City Kansas Mall

Number of Blocks	Date of Completion	Funding Type	Cost	Sales Increase (Yes or No)
6	1967	Assessment district and private	$ 964,000	Yes
6	1964	Assessment district and urban renewal	$ 1,600,000	Yes, then leveled off
3	1974	Federal	1,500,000	N.A.
6		Neighborhood Development	$ 8,000,000	
3	1969	Urban renewal	$ 653,000	Yes
9	1963	Improvement district and city	$ 682,000	Yes
2½	1974	Federal and local	$ 1,600,000	Yes
6	1977	N.A.	N.A.	Yes
4	1966	City assessment and private funds	$ 730,107	Yes, then down
9	1969	Assessment district and federal	$ 3,600,000	N.A.
3	1965	Assessment district and city	$ 675,550	Yes
6	1973	Urban Renewal and New London Association, state	$ 1,426,209	N.A.
6	1976	City bonds	$ 1,500,000	Yes
1 2	1976	Urban renewal	$ 6,300,000	N.A.
8	1960	Municipal bonds	$ 600,000	Yes
5	1974	City, federal, and donations	$ 533,954	Yes
1	1971	Urban renewal and city	$ 1,800,000	Yes
6	1969	Private, Board of Water Supply, city and county	$ 2,766,450	Yes
1	1970	Special assessment	$ 33,955	N.A.
2	1967	Assessment district and city	$ 112,000	Yes
3½	1970	Special assessment	$ 530,000	N.A.
2	1968	Assessment owners and merchants, private	$ 120,000	N.A.
4	1975	Urban renewal and merchants	$ 890,000	No
3	1971	Assessments and city	$ 565,000	Yes
7	1971	City, assessment district, and federal	$ 1,000,000	Yes
4	1969	Assessment district	$ 494,000	N.A.
4	1972	Urban renewal and merchants	$ 750,000	Yes
2 3	1977	Community Development and Neighborhood Development	$ 3,000,000	N.A.
8	1971	Federal and local	$ 1,400,000	N.A.
2½	1964	City and urban renewal	$ 3,600,000	Yes
3	1971	Urban renewal and city	$ 2,300,000	No

Location	Population	Type	Name
Parsons, Kansas	13,015	Full	Parsons Plaza
Frankfort, Kentucky	21,902	Full	St. Clair Mall
Louisville, Kentucky	361,706	Full	River City Mall
Lake Charles, Louisiana	77,998	Full	Downtown Mall
Portland, Maine	65,116	Full	Maine Way Mall
Baltimore, Maryland	905,759	Full	Lexington Street Mall
Baltimore, Maryland	905,759	Full	Oldtown Mall
Salisbury, Maryland	15,252	Full	Downtown Salisbury Plaza
New Bedford, Massachusetts	101,777	Full	Downtown Mall
Newburyport, Massachusetts	15,807	Full	Inn Street Mall
Salem, Massachusetts	40,556	Full	Essex Mall
Battle Creek, Michigan	38,931	Full and semi	Michigan Mall
East Lansing, Michigan	47,540	Full	East Lansing Mall
Jackson, Michigan	45,484	Full	Progress Place
Kalamazoo, Michigan	85,555	Full	The Kalamazoo Mall
Lansing, Michigan	131,403	Full	Washington Square Mall
Minneapolis, Minnesota	434,400	Transit	Nicollet Mall
Winona, Minnesota	26,438	Full	Levee Plaza
Helena, Montana	22,730	Full	Last Chance Mall
Lincoln, Nebraska	149,518	Full	Centennial Mall
Lebanon, New Hampshire	9,725	Full	Lebanon Downtown Mall
Atlantic City, New Jersey	47,859	Semi	Gordon's Alley
Cape May, New Jersey	4,392	Full	Washington Street Mall
Patterson, New Jersey	144,824	Full	Lower Main Street Mall
Trenton, New Jersey	104,786	Full	Trenton Commons
Las Cruces, New Mexico	37,857	Full	Las Cruces Downtown Mall
Auburn, New York	34,599	Full	State Street Mall
Ithaca, New York	26,226	Full	Ithaca Commons
Poughkeepsie, New York	32,029	Full	Main Street Mall
Greenville, North Carolina	29,063	Transit	Downtown Greenville Mall
Monroe, North Carolina	11,282	Full	Courthouse Plaza
Raleigh, North Carolina	147,273	Full	Exchange Street Mall
Winston-Salem, North Carolina	133,683	Full	Downtown Walkway
Middletown, Ohio	48,767	Full	Middletown Mall
Painesville, Ohio	16,536	Full	Main Street Mall
Youngstown, Ohio	140,909	Full	Youngstown Federal Plaza
Coos Bay, Oregon	13,466	Full	Coos Bay Mall
Eugene, Oregon	79,028	Full	City Center Mall
Portland, Oregon	379,967	Transit	Portland Transit Mall
Allentown, Pennsylvania	109,572	Semi	Hamilton Mall
Erie, Pennsylvania	130,084	Transit	Downtown Mall
Germantown, Philadelphia, Penn.	1,861,719	Full	Maplewood Mall
Philadelphia, Pennsylvania	1,861,719	Transit	Chestnut Street Transitway
Pittsburgh, Pennsylvania	520,089	Full and transit	East Liberty Mall
Pottsville, Pennsylvania	19,715	Full	Centre Street Mall
Reading, Pennsylvania	84,097	Full and semi	Penn Square
Scranton, Pennsylvania	103,564	Semi	Wyoming Avenue Mini-Mall

Number of Blocks	Date of Completion	Funding Type	Cost	Sales Increase (Yes or No)
4	1971	Federal and local	$ 850,000	Yes
1	1975	Federal Neighborhood Development	$ 325,000	No
3	1973	Assessment, urban renewal, and bonds	$ 1,713,000	Yes
4	1970	Assessment district, city, private	$ 650,000	N.A.
5	1975	Federal and city	$ 2,225,000	N.A.
2	1974	City	$ 800,000	Yes
2	1976	Urban renewal and Community Development	$ 2,600,000	N.A.
2	1968	City and merchants	$ 165,000	N.A.
3	1974	Revenue sharing and private	$ 495,000	N.A.
4	1975	Federal Highway, urban renewal, and state	$ 2,500,000	Yes
4	1977	Urban renewal	$ 1,000,000	N.A.
4	1975	Special assessment and local	$ 2,000,000	Yes
2	1970–1975	City, utilities and, merchants	$ 312,000	N.A.
3	1965	Local contributor	$ 80,000	No
2	1959	Assessment district	$ 82,348	Yes
3	1973	Urban renewal	$ 850,000	N.A.
8	1967	Federal and assessments	$ 3,875,000	Yes
3	1969	Assessment and donations	$ 225,000	N.A.
4	1974	Urban renewal	$ 417,414	N.A.
7	1970	City, assessment, private, federal	$ 603,775	N.A.
1	1968	Urban renewal and city	$ 450,000	Yes
½	1973	Private	$ 1,500,000	Yes
3	1971	Urban renewal	$ 1,500,000	Yes
1	1974	Urban renewal	$ 568,000	N.A.
2	1974	City, federal, state, and assessment	$ 1,800,000	Leveled off
7	1972	Urban renewal and city	$ 1,200,000	N.A.
1	1977	Community Development	$ 170,000	N.A.
3	1975	City assessments	$ 1,130,000	Yes
3	1973	Urban renewal, city and state	$ 3,200,000	Leveled off
2	1975	Urban renewal	$ 425,000	Yes
3	1976	Urban renewal and local	$ 280,000	N.A.
3½	1977	Downtown tax district, city, county, and state	$ 2,000,000	N.A.
8	1975	Urban renewal and city	$ 1,500,000	Yes
2	1974	Federal Neighborhood Development	$ 6,000,000	N.A.
1	1973	Street improvement utilities funds	$ 143,045	No
3	1974	Bonds by city	$ 1,832,700	N.A.
3	1970	Assessments and urban renewal	$ 2,000,000	Yes
5	1971	Urban renewal and city	$ 1,350,000	N.A.
22	1977	Urban Mass Transportation Administration, Tri-met	$15,000,000	Yes
4	1973	State and bonds	$ 5,000,000	Yes
4	1974	Federal, state, and city	$ 1,600,000	N.A.
2	1974	Urban renewal, city redevelopment	$ 500,000	Yes
12	1976	Urban Mass Transportation Administration	$ 7,400,000	N.A.
14	1974	Federal and local community development	$ 3,585,000	Yes
7	1977	State, community affairs, city	$ 1,250,000	N.A.
2	1975	State, city, assessment, and county	$ 1,600,000	N.A.
1	1978	Community Development, Economic Development Administration, and merchants	$ 862,000	N.A.

Location	Population	Type	Name
Wilkes-Barre, Pennsylvania	58,856	Semi	Downtown Pedestrian Canopy and Mall
Williamsport, Pennsylvania	37,918	Full Semi	Center City Mall
Providence, Rhode Island	179,116	Full	Westminster Mall
Greenville, South Carolina	61,436	Full	Coffee Street Mall
Spartanburg, South Carolina	44,546	Full	Main Street Mall
Knoxville, Tennessee	188,470	Full	Market Square Mall
Memphis, Tennessee	623,530	Full	Mid-America Mall
Dallas, Texas	844,401	Full	Stoneplace Mall
Dallas, Texas	844,401	Semi	Akard Street Mall
Galveston, Texas	61,809	Full	Central Plaza
Charlottesville, Virginia	38,880	Full	Main Street Mall
Seattle, Washington	530,831	Full	Occidental Mall
Tacoma, Washington	157,000	Full	Broadway Street Plaza
Sheboygan, Wisconsin	50,000	Full	Plaza 8
Ottawa, Ontario, Canada	365,921	Full	Sparks Street Mall
Quebec City, Quebec, Canada	187,833	Full	St. Roch Mall
Vancouver, British Columbia, Canada	426,520	Transit	Granville Mall

Number of Blocks	Date of Completion	Funding Type	Cost	Sales Increase (Yes or No)
2	1977	Federal and state	$ 2,300,000	N.A.
2	1976	Special assessment district	$ 1,500,000	N.A.
8				
6	1965	City, federal, and private	$ 530,000	N.A.
1	1975	Urban renewal and private	$ 274,000	Yes
2	1975	General revenue sharing funds	$ 750,000	N.A.
1	1961	City and private	$ 313,000	Yes
12	1976	Tax assessments	$ 6,000,000	N.A.
1	1965	City	$ 110,000	N.A.
3	1974	City, capital improvements bonds	$ 890,000	N.A.
2	1970	City and assessment	$ 160,000	N.A.
5	1976	City capital improvements and assessments	$ 2,000,000	Yes
2	1973	City and federal	$ 750,000	N.A.
2	1976	Urban renewal	$ 1,500,000	Yes
3½	1976	Urban renewal and local	$ 1,600,000	Yes
3	1967	Assessment and city	$ 636,000	Yes
5	1974	City, federal, provincial	$ 4,700,000	Yes
6	1974	Property owners, federal, city, utilities	$ 2,947,000	N.A.

Bibliography

Alexander, Laurence A., *Downtown Malls, An Annual Review,* Volume 2, New York, Downtown Research and Development Center, 1976.

Aschman, Frederick T., "Nicollet Mall: Civic Cooperation to Preserve Downtown's Vitality," *Planners Notebook,* September, 1971.

Bernatzky, Aloys, "Climatic Influences of Greens and City Planning," *Anthos,* No. 1, 1966.

Bernatzky, Aloys, "The Performance and Value of Trees," *Anthos,* No. 1, 1969.

Carpenter, Philip L., Theodore D. Walker, and Frederick O. Lanphear, *Plants in the Landscape,* San Francisco, W. H. Freeman and Company, 1975.

Carr, Stephen, Ashley/Myer/Smith, *City Signs and Lights,* for Boston Redevelopment Authority, Cambridge, M.I.T. Press, 1973.

Chamberlain, Gary M., "Bring New Vitality to Main Street," *The American City,* November, 1969.

Darlow, Arthur E., "Miami to Upgrade the Downtown," *The American City,* August, 1959.

Eimon, Pan Dodd, "The City Tells Its Story," *The American City,* November, 1960.

Elliott, C. H., "Long-Term Benefits of a Shoppers' Mall," *The American City,* March, 1964.

Faull, Harry A., "Pomona Sets a Pattern," *The American City,* January, 1964.

Fruin, John J., *Pedestrian Planning and Design,* New York, Metropolitan Association of Urban Designers and Environmental Planners, Inc., 1977.

Gruen, Victor, *Centers for the Urban Environment,* New York, Van Nostrand Reinhold Company, 1973.

Haimback, David, "The Fresno Mall," *The American City,* April, 1965.

Howell, Richard L., "The Untapped Urban Resource," *Parks and Recreation,* September, 1975.

Kemmerer, Harleigh, "Managing Outdoor Lighting," *Grounds Maintenance,* 1976.

Kozel, P. C., "Superior Trees for Landscaping," *Landscape Industry,* February/March, 1975.

Lynch, Kevin, *The Image of the City,* Cambridge, M.I.T. Press, 1960.

Malt, Harold L., *Furnishing the City,* New York, McGraw-Hill Book Company, 1970.

Martin, Roger, "Exciting Start with Nicollet Mall," *Landscape Architecture,* July, 1969.

Nelson, Carl, "How Main St., Evansville, Came Alive," *The American City,* November, 1973.

Redstone, Louis G., *The New Downtowns: Rebuilding Business Districts,* New York, McGraw-Hill Book Company, 1976.

Robinette, Gary O., *Plants/People/ and Environmental Quality,* Washington, D.C., U.S. Department of the Interior, National Park Service, in collaboration with the American Society of Landscape Architects Foundation, 1972.

Robinette, Margaret A., *Outdoor Sculpture: Object and Environment,* New York, Whitney Library of Design, 1976.

Rubenstein, Harvey M., *A Guide To Site and Environmental Planning,* New York, John Wiley and Sons, 1969.

Schlivek, Louis B., "Four Places Where Urban Design and Planning Are Paying Dividends," *A.I.A. Journal,* August, 1975.

Williams, Alva, Jr., "Free Parking in Downtown? You're Kidding!" *Traffic Engineering,* June, 1975.

Winslow, Joan, "Semimall Brings Shoppers Back to Town," *The American City,* February, 1974.

Wyman, Donald, *Trees for American Gardens,* New York, The Macmillan Company, 1951.

Zion, Robert L., *Trees for Architecture and the Landscape,* New York, Reinhold Publishing Corporation, 1968.

Index